An Agile Life

Author: Vishal K. Wadhwani

Edition: 1

Year: 2020

Language: English

PUBLISHING HISTORY

KINDLE EDITION PUBLISHED JULY 2020

PAPERBACK EDITION PUBLISHED AUGUST 2020

If you wish to use the content and materials inside this book to improve the productivity of your teams, please contact the author, no strings attached.

Amazon Author Page - amazon.com/author/vishalww

LinkedIn Page - linkedin.com/in/vishalwadhwani

Web Page - anagile.team

Disclaimer

The principles of this book have been based on a global and public known methodology called Agile and based on the Manifesto for Agile Software Development, created by several representatives from the software development industry in 2001, and whose references you may find at agilemanifesto.org. This book's intention is to contribute in a complementary manner to this methodology to guide leaders on different practices and approaches to this methodology, providing examples, experiences, and a practical approach to solving modern and ambiguous problems within global organizations.

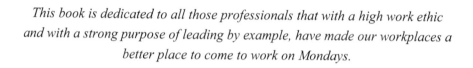

This book is dedicated to all those professionals that with a high work ethic and with a strong purpose of leading by example, have made our workplaces a better place to come to work on Mondays.

And to my parents and sister, without whom I couldn't have learnt the value of surrounding yourself by humble, selfless people.

CONTENTS

LET ME GIVE YOU SOME CONTEXT 11

CASE I. HOW TO FALL IN LOVE WITH AGILE...................14

I AM IN A MISSION TO KILL GANTT CHARTS..................19

THE APPLICABLE PRINCIPLES OF AGILE METHODOLOGY 21

WHAT DEFINITELY IS NOT AGILE...............................25

CASE II. SMALL DOSES, BETTER THAN A HUGE DEVIATION...........26

THE SCRUM CONCEPT 30

THE PLAYBOOK 39

BALANCING DONE VS PERFECT...............................49

COFFEE BREAK! 54

AGILE LIFE I. HIGH LEVEL GOALS AND PROJECTS 55

CASE III. MAKE IT HARD TO STOP RATHER THAN HARD TO START59

SPRINT I 65

TIPS FOR EFFECTIVE DAILY MEETINGS 83

BREAK CHAPTER...............................89

SPRINT II 92

CASE IV. AGILE ENABLING SERVANT LEADERSHIP 111

SPRINT III 117

CASE V. OUTPUTS VS OUTCOMES...............................135

SPRINT IV 139

PERFORMANCE TRACKING 152

CONCLUSION...............................157

COMMITMENT TO QUALITY 159

ABOUT THE AUTHOR 162

LET ME GIVE YOU SOME CONTEXT

Let me give you some context. We are recovering from a world-wide pandemic that has been brutal, not only to the health of many but also to our economy and daily life. If change had already become the new normal, rapid change will become the new normal after this global crisis. Thus, it will become crucial to handle professional projects in ways that allows us to change priorities, pivot, adapt quickly to changes in the environment, get the feeling that we are moving forward and getting things done, and focusing on delivering value and not just delivering for the sake of saying something is done. With this situation, time will become more valuable and the desire to spend it in tasks that have a purpose and that really add value will influence many of our corporate decisions on what to do first, what doesn't add value anymore and what needs to be done to ensure the projects we run are bringing tangible business value.

During the last few months, I have tried to apply the principles of a very well-known IT methodology to some of my personal projects to see how it felt and how much I was able to get done. The goal was not only to try a different approach to handling personal projects but also to prove that this methodology could be used in many different areas inside any company that feels the need to achieve better results, deliver value to stakeholders, adapt its business decisions constantly, achieve valuable outcomes, great team spirit, and a strong sense of satisfaction. This same book has been published leveraging Agile Methodologies which means I am constantly improving it and gathering feedback in order to deliver more value on each new version.

Why do I think this methodology can help in different areas rather than just being a typical methodology for software development? Because of its principles, the way they fit the current reality, the way they apply to modern organizations, and because it has worked in different situations, for instance, Operational teams or Sales teams. Agile is a very dynamic methodology, usually underestimated by the industry since it is only known to be used in IT teams, but it is extremely powerful to manage teams in different areas or departments that liaise with stakeholders, have a changing environment, and want to handle changing priorities quickly and effectively delivering value iteratively. The fun part is that these principles can also be applied to modern lifestyle, and this is how the book can help you infer the potential of Agile methodology to handle both personal and professional projects, regardless of their size.

In the past projects were linear, delivered upon planning and it had usually one main stakeholder that would benefit from it, these projects never handled changes in business from the planning to the implementation and never handled corner cases correctly, this would always result in delays, lack of expectation management and delivering products that needed new improvements that would result in newer projects, that used to work, but now, when change is constantly happening, when business are constantly pivoting, and when stakeholders are constantly demanding transparency about the status of any project that impacts them, Agile Methodologies can be a near to perfect solution to help companies become more nimble and adapt quickly their projects to new situations.

The goal of this book is to help both you, your team and your stakeholders, regardless of the department in which you work or the type of job you do. In any project where you need to deliver value, gather feedback, liaise constantly with stakeholders and provide transparency about what is going on, this book intends to help you from a practical perspective to manage these variables in an effective manner. We are using real situations that I have faced during my career in order to introduce the context and be able to infer the concept. To exemplify the project, we will use personal goals to which we will apply Agile principles to get them moving forward and, throughout the book, I will share cases, tips, and templates that will help you put together this awesome methodology for your projects. It is important to point out that the book is completely practical, I won't spend more than a chapter talking about Agile's principles, since they are easy to understand and what will make the different is the practical approach of this methodology when executing projects.

Between chapters, I include extra concepts, tips, or interesting applications that are very useful when applying Agile methodologies and that have been learnt and proven through experience, these are not part of the core knowledge of the methodology but are equally important to make this methodology work.

For instance, stakeholder management, prioritizing tasks, tips for daily meetings, dealing with procrastination or dispersion of the team, and, last but not least, performance tracking.

CASE 1. HOW TO FALL IN LOVE WITH AGILE

It was January, not the best weather I must say, and I was asking myself if the weather had something to do with how tired and exhausted, I was feeling. It was raining, too, and everything looked grayish outside.

We were in a conference room inside the headquarters of what was one of our biggest clients in Europe. The client was scolding our boss, and our boss was trying to flip the guilt around. Classic, it is kind of funny when you think about it years later.

- *"This deliverable falls way below what I expected to see"* - our client claimed.

- *"We have delivered what was planned and confirmed by email. We have had tremendous delays due to part of the other team not handling the information we needed. These dependencies have affected the timeline, but the deliverable is what we agreed to upfront."* - my boss replied.

I actually hadn't seen both of them talking to each other in weeks, even months. Had they been following up? Did we fail as a team to escalate issues? We had been very thorough in doing exactly what was confirmed on paper, so that they couldn't accuse us of not doing our part. Was there a mismatch of expectations? I really didn't know if the situation had changed and our deliverable now didn't add the expected value. I did know we did everything that had been agreed upon. Now I understand that it wasn't enough; alignment and expectation management had fallen short during this project.

- *"Hey Christine, what now?* - I asked to my senior colleague

---

- *"To be honest, I think they both had a point. We will probably ask for more time and include a few of their new requests in order to accommodate changes in business and processes, but part of the work we have done will fall through the cracks. Don't worry, a few more weeks doing overtime, we'll survive."* - she replied. She had already worked on other projects with this client.

After having some difficult conversations with our client, we agreed to start scheduling "demo" meetings with our business and operational stakeholders to show the outcomes of our work and gather feedback regarding any project requirement that would be subject to change. When we finished the assessment, we realized that 20% of the requirements were obsolete. Some business processes had improved during this period and a good number of the new features were not solving some of the issues and pain points that our stakeholders had been suffering with for some time. This meant another two or three months of rework and a very upset client; we weren't happy either.

We had used the ***Waterfall*** project management approach, which is a linear methodology for project management which divides each project into; requirement gathering (As-Is model), design (To-Be model), development, testing, and deployment.

What happened here? Let me give you my perspective.

- The As-Is model was probably done by a person on our team that wasn't an expert on the processes and procedures that we were trying to improve. That means that no matter how much time and effort he or she dedicated to gathering information about the process, he or she would never have the same knowledge as a person that actually did the task every single day. Keeping strings attached to these people and gathering feedback regularly would have helped increase the quality and impact of the project.

- The As-Is model was prepared with an old scenario, probably more than six months old, and didn't acknowledge the possibility of changes, which in the rapidly changing environment that we live in today could have been unrealistic. Six months can be a lot of time in the environment we work in today because organizational reality and market trends change rapidly.

- The As-Is model wasn't validated in a way that would allow everybody impacted by the model to provide feedback. Most likely, what happened during this phase is that managers reviewed the documents very quickly, made comments based on their knowledge, and decided to approve without double checking every single case with each of the persons that handled these tasks individually. As a result, issues did not arise on time to have them considered for the project.

- The nature of the project, gathering requirements at the beginning and then delivering the project, had nothing to do with the reality of the business where it is crucial to keep talking regularly with your stakeholders to understand their expectations and agree on deadlines and priorities.

- The project wasn't subject to any kind of inspection or intermediate checks from those that would end up using our work. There was not a proper feedback system in place between us and the real users, which I have come to believe is crucial for successful rollouts.

I could go on and on analyzing more issues on the way tasks were executed but there is no point in doing this because, to be honest, many of these points are real pain points in different projects and across industries. Some of them are difficult to avoid and blaming anyone would just be ineffective. The key takeaways are, expectations weren't met, rework had to be done, and the perceived value of our work ended up being lower compared to the effort (and overtime) that was put in place.

A few years later, I started working on another project with very similar characteristics, but it felt totally different. They had changed the structure of their projects to reduce the amount of time spent in documentation, they had reduced the time to market from definition to testing and inspection, and they had put in place a shorter feedback cycle. The client checked our work every two weeks and didn't expect perfection but, rather, a viable product or piece of work upon which they could provide feedback so that we could improve during the next cycle of two weeks. Plans and expectations were revised every two weeks, feedback was gathered almost every day, the methodology had been imported from the US and it sounded fancy, Scrum Agile they called it. The most impressive part for me was that people were not working overtime any more to deliver on time and within quality. Believe me, in that industry, that was something difficult to achieve and it was difficult for me to believe at first, call me skeptical.

I went to my first daily stand-up meeting (we will talk about this later in the book), and to my surprise one of the questions that each one of us would answer in that meeting was: *"What is getting in your way or keeping you from doing your job?"*

I now believe that this is one of the most powerful questions a leader can ask. They proactively encouraged everybody to put any problem or roadblock on the table so that we could tackle it as a team, together. They had put in place the environment for every single person in the room to be able to speak up and openly talk about any risk that would impede delivering with the quality that was expected. With this powerful question, they generated a sense of self-accountability for each one of us by talking openly and transparently about our duties and the issues we faced to deliver them.

I fell in love. I then felt kind of nerdy, you know, after falling in love with a methodology.

Something that surprised me is that the planning was really democratic, for each task we would be able to make our own estimations on how much it would take to get it done and the whole team would estimate and then reach an agreement on how much time it would take to get it done. This generated a sense of self-accountability and encouraged everybody to arrive prepared to meetings, but also allowed us to have a say in planning and not be hit by insane deadlines and unbearable scopes. Planning, meetings, insane deadlines, and many others have always been painful issues in projects executed in different industries with a high tech component, I felt Agile Methodologies could be put to a better use if we would apply them to any team that ran project based and had to manage expectations, execute quickly, deliver to internal clients and improve based on their feedback.

I AM IN A MISSION TO KILL GANTT CHARTS

Let's compare how project were done in the past and how they are done now.

	Projects in the past	Current Projects
Planning	Had to be done previously, thoroughly and meticulously in order to allocate resources	Needs to be done on the go due to changes in the company and business environment
	Usually done at the beginning without changes during execution	If planning is performed long before execution, changes in eco-system will result in replanning and rework
	Linear planning where each phase couldn't begin without completing the previous one	Module planning where tasks can be executed in parallel, phases can be started while completing previous ones and desire to make tasks independant one from another to encourage team autonomy
Stakeholders	Usually one main stakeholder impacted	Usually more than one stakeholder impacted or needed to build the final product
	Very few interactions usually at the beginning, touchpoints and final stages of the project	Constant interaction to exchange information, align expectations, work together on discoveries and collaborate to build the final product
	Formal communication channels	Informal or practical communication channels
	Usually demanded their requirements	Negotiation of requirements based on each others resources available
	Usually didn't require updates on status since they assumed everything was according to what was planned unless formal communication of delays	Wants to know the status of the project to address any impact in their groups of interests
Tasks	Defined at the beginning and rarely changed, any changes would result in rework, realignment and a whole process of approvals	Changing every month
	Unrelated to high level business goals	Strongly depending on a business goal and linked through OKRs or targets
	Only known by the team and project managers	Usually known by different stakeholders who are interacting with the team to get things done
People Management	Team working overtime to reach deadlines	People are encouraged to estimate based on their knowledge on how much will realisticly take to get the job done
	Leaders weren't held accountable for poor team morale	Leaders now have performance targets related to the team's wellbeing
	Results more important than people	People management and results equally important during execution
	Stakeholders were handled by project managers or points of contact inside the project	Anybody in the team can connect with stakeholders

THE APPLICABLE PRINCIPLES OF AGILE METHODOLOGY

The Agile Methodology can be perceived in two ways:

- as a project management methodology, or

- as a cultural approach to project development based on people, values, and tools.

Both can be useful depending on the situation. For instance, if you are working tight on time in a small project that is being handled by external contractors and you want to focus on execution, the methodology can be used to track progress and organize the workload more efficiently among the team in order to increase the value delivered and maximize the return on investment. But, if you are managing a team, or you belong to a team in an organization, you should be inclined to use the second approach in order to leverage the methodology to its fullest, in order not only to only execute but also to generate the environment that allows professionals to succeed, adapt to change, successfully engage with their eco-system, and in general, come to work happier, which will provide much needed value to your organization.

Agile was born in Utah, around 2001 when several representatives from different programming methodologies gathered together to develop the Agile Manifesto and the creation of a global Agile Alliance to help others in the industry think about the best methods and approaches that could be used for agile, nimble, and effective software development in current changing scenarios. You can find more information about it on the official Agile website, agilemanifesto.org, but we are going to focus on some of its most important principles that can help you understand the potential of the methodology.

Agile Principles[1]. **the words I would like you to focus on are in bold and underlined**:

- **Our highest priority is to satisfy the customer through early and continuous delivery** of valuable software.

- **Welcome changing requirements**, even late in development. **Agile processes harness change** for the customer's competitive advantage.

- **Deliver** working software **frequently**, from a couple of weeks to a couple of months, **with a preference for the shorter timescale**.

- **Business people and developers must work together daily throughout the project.**

- **Build projects around motivated individuals. Give them the environment and support they need, and trust them** to get the job done.

- The most efficient and effective method of conveying information to and within a development team is through face-to-face conversation.

- Working software is the primary measure of progress.

- Agile processes promote sustainable development. The sponsors, developers, and users should be able to maintain a constant pace indefinitely.

- Continuous attention to technical excellence and good design enhances agility.

- **Simplicity**--the art of maximizing the amount of work not done--is essential.

- **The best** architectures, **requirements, and designs emerge from self-organizing teams.**

- **At regular intervals, the team reflects on how to become more effective, then fine tunes and adjusts its behavior accordingly.**

[1] Source: *Agile Alliance, www.agilealliance.org*

The key takeaways to make the most of this methodology for your projects (personal projects too) are:

- Allow your goals and tasks to evolve and adapt as needed to the environment. One of the core values of this methodology is the fact that it is prepared to deliver in a rapidly changing environment. Don't be afraid to add new tasks, lower a task's priority, or increase a task's priority. You are allowed and encouraged to do so if it is going to help you maximize the effectiveness of your time. You want to deliver small portions of what you want to achieve frequently and continuously. There is no need to build a huge thing which often can lead to procrastination. Separate the different tasks of your project into small pieces and try to add one or two of these pieces to each cycle.

- Allow yourself to change priorities, sometimes you won't feel like doing a task, or the task depends on an external factor, or you are not in the mood, allow yourself to stop this task and start another one from the list of small tasks that you want to tackle in one cycle, be open to re-prioritizing tasks.

- Evaluate and inspect your work every end of cycle and decide what you want to prioritize for the next cycle, based on the environment, priorities, roadblocks, and dependencies.

- At regular intervals, self-evaluate, decide what you need to improve, not only in what you are doing but how you are doing it, and implement improvements in the next cycle.

- The goal should be to deliver value through incremental work, that way you can reduce the amount of rework and re-evaluate or pivot when necessary without setting yourself up for a huge deviation of budget.

- Do not complicate things, try and define what you want to achieve in a simple manner, don't set the bar too high just for one single task.

WHAT DEFINITELY IS NOT AGILE

After having gone through the Methodology's values and principles Let's address what is definitely not Agile. Some of the following aspects should be polished in order to actually achieve their goal of being an Agile friendly company:

- Having endless and unstructured meetings

- Meetings without an agenda

- Deadlines stablished without a negotiation process with the team where impact, requirements and necessary information is analyzed

- Not linking tasks to projects that align with high level goals, assigning random tasks that have little to do with the teams' goals

- Spending more time on presentations than what might be productive and effective

- Improving ways that stakeholders can get transparency on any project that impacts them

CASE II. SMALL DOSES, BETTER THAN A HUGE DEVIATION

I was really intrigued. The conversation had shifted from personal stuff like where we liked to travel to the company she had built with a good friend. It was really interesting since she was talking with a passion I didn't usually see in my circles. Most of the people I had interviewed during my trip to London were professionals that weren't even thinking about going on their own to build a company. They were very comfortable receiving a stable paycheck, so being able to interview a professional that had actually stepped out of this comfort zone and had been able to experience what it was like to build her own company was kind of refreshing. She started talking about how she had come to the idea and why she had started to build the product. During all our conversations, I couldn't help thinking that even though the idea was interesting I really wanted to know how she was able to develop the product without having any technical knowledge, so I decided to ask her and then the conversation started getting more intense.

She explained to me how this specific part of the project had been a real pain point and how it had drained resources and energy from the whole project. What had happened is that she outsourced the development of the app to an app studio in Europe and even though they had delivered on time and it was the product that supposedly was agreed to, she felt the final product didn't meet her expectations. The design wasn't as appealing as she expected for the price she paid and the requirements were met to a minimum level. There were a lot of compromises from her side to make the product viable, corner cases weren't taken into consideration, many of the quality tests were done without taking into consideration the real customer journey. So she felt they didn't test the functionality as it was going to be used by the user but only that the technical development worked correctly. The feeling was that they had tested the technical stuff but never tested the real business feature to make sure it worked and it was intuitive for any user. She sued them, of course, but since the app studio had previous negotiation experience, they were able to defend their work, which resulted in her feeling she had wasted so much money on a product that wasn't 100% up to the job plus legal fees. This took so much optimism away from the project. I guess in this story we can see the power of execution to define the success of a good idea.

Let's show this issue in a simple chart. This example shows a project defined in week 1 and delivered in week 15:

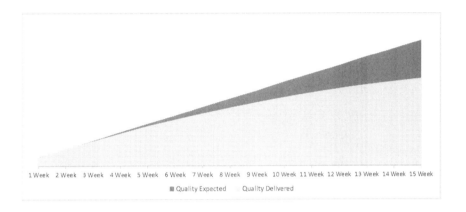

The dark area could be caused by the following:
- Lack of communication between the team doing the work and the product owner or requester
- Lack of answering the questions, why? for what? what is expected to be seen? how is it expected to work from a business perspective?
- Lack of expectation management from the supplier (or the team doing the work)
- Ineffective testing, having to re-do all the testing
- Corner cases overlooked

The dark area could result in the following:
- Potential rework
- Reduction of the ROI
- Increasing distrust from the client (or internal stakeholder)

- Frustration of team members
- Potential legal issues
- Potential overtime for both teams

Even if we had decided to add a checkpoint in week 7 or 8, the final deviation wouldn't change much from the chart above because usually these checks are made in a superficial manner and without inspection.

Now, let's see how this would look applying some Agile principles:

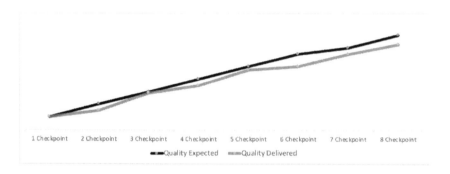

In order to achieve this quality progression, we would need to make sure that we foster the following:

- Checkpoints every two weeks (between 2-4 weeks is considered appropriate)
- Daily meetings to talk about progress and what is expected
- Effective task description, where we explain the definition of done and what is expected to be seen
- Talk about the goal of each deliverable
- Effective communication and effective follow-up from both sides, with the client being the one who proactively seeks updates (The old approach, I pay you, tell you what to do, and we will see each other in a few months doesn't work anymore).
- Feedback sessions where pivoting and priority changes are allowed
- Effective inspection of the work done and not just high-level validations

THE SCRUM CONCEPT

One of the most important applications of Agile principles is the Scrum Agile Methodology[2]. They are both linked to each other, Agile is the baseline and Scrum is the variation that makes those principles work in a certain business environment. The Scrum approach to Agile Methodology is a combination of roles, tools or artifacts, meetings, and values, which when combined result in a powerful self-organizing project management culture. These methods break work into small pieces that minimize the amount of planning and design needed to deliver a piece of work. Also, it prioritizes a short feedback cycle which allows time to adapt quickly to any changes needed to make any piece of work as valuable as possible for the real current needs of the business.

A very important concept to start understanding the methodology is the Sprint (sometimes called time-box), which is the time that runs from the first day of the cycle to the last day, usually between 2-4 weeks, depending on different variables that we will discuss further in this book. Now, let's start talking about these tools, meetings, roles, and values, starting with the latter.

Values and examples on how they can be applied[3]:

Value	Application example

---

[2] Source: *Agile Alliance, www.agilealliance.org*

[3] Source: *Scrum Alliance Values, https://www.scrumalliance.org/about-scrum/values*

Commitment. Scrum teams work together as a unit. This means that Scrum and Agile teams trust each other to follow through on what they say they are going to do. When team members aren't sure how work is going, they ask. Agile teams only agree to take on tasks they believe they can complete, so they are careful not to overcommit.	**Example 1.** A very important approach to this is not overcommitting about what you are able to get done, since the foundation of the principle is trust, trust that the person who said he is going to do something actually does it. **Example 2.** You shouldn't take it as intrusiveness if team members want to understand the current status of the task you are working on. It is not distrust, it is transparency as long as it's bidirectional. **Example 3.** The team works together, never against each other or stepping over each other, with a collaborative approach.
Courage. Teams must feel safe enough to say no, to ask for help, and to try new things. Agile teams must be brave enough to question the status quo when it hampers their ability to succeed.	**Example 1.** Imagine you have agreed that certain tasks will be delivered within a deadline, and an important stakeholder asks you for something additional. The team must be comfortable to either say no, or let the stakeholder know that if a new task is added another task with similar time cost has to fall to the next cycle. This is extremely usual when the team is dealing with different stakeholders at the same time. **Example 2.** Senior people on the team must encourage people with less experience to speak up, and not to be afraid to have difficult conversations (always with respect and empathy). Leaders must encourage people to speak their minds in order to tackle frictions that may arise. **Example 3.** Scrum Masters or Agile Coaches must help the team negotiate with stakeholders whenever needed in order to ensure the wellbeing of the team.
Focus. Whatever Scrum teams start, they finish--so Agile teams are relentless about limiting the amount of work in process (limit	**Example 1.** For each task, we need to agree on a definition of "done." This will be the definition that will keep the team on track and focused on the

WIP).	outcome expected. **Example 2.** Encouraging the team to work on small tasks at a time and only pause them or start another one if there is a dependency. Multi-tasking is not banned but not considered to be better than focusing on something and finishing it.
Openness. Teams consistently seek out new ideas and opportunities to learn. Agile teams are also honest when they need help.	**Example 1.** The team is encouraged constantly to talk about any problem that is stopping them from getting the job done, in an open and safe space. **Example 2.** Meetings like "the retrospective" encourage team members to talk openly about pain points and how to improve the way the team operates and deals with stakeholders. **Example 3.** The team is encouraged to raise shortcomings of previous development or critical improvements they feel need to get done. The quicker this is raised the better.
Respect. Team members demonstrate respect to one another, to the Product Owner, to stakeholders, and to the Scrum Master. Agile teams know that their strength lies in how well they collaborate, and that everyone has a distinct contribution to make toward completing the work of the Sprint.	**Example 1.** Respect each other's ideas, give each other permission to have a bad day once in a while. **Example 2.** Recognize each other's accomplishments.

Roles and Responsibilities[4]

Scrum Master

Profile	Functions
- Effective communicator - Influencer - Listens - Encourages collaboration over competition - People manager	- Facilitates and drives meetings - Leads without authority, behind the scenes, to make sure the team stays focused - Makes sure the methodology runs smoothly - Reinforces Agile principles through the organization
	Responsible For...
	- Owning and driving all Agile meetings - Helping on the maintenance of Agile tools - Removing impediments from the team - Exploring and finding techniques to improve the methodology, such as new retrospective meetings or new ways to manage the Product Backlog

---

[4] Source: *Scrum Alliance, https://www.scrumalliance.org/*

Product Owner

Profile	Functions
- Effective stakeholder manager - Business savvy - Persuasive - Accessible to the team - Low-level knowledge - Autonomous, is able to make decisions about the direction and goals of the projects	- Designs the team's goals and high-level direction - Aligns the team's goals to the corporation's objectives - Prioritizes according to the company's targets and makes sure stakeholders are heard - Represents the internal and external customers' needs
	Responsible For...
	- Defining the goal of each Sprint (cycle) - Defining the tasks inside the Product Backlog - Deciding priorities for each Sprint (cycle) - Supporting the team in questions related to the Product Backlog and tasks - Approving the tasks delivered by the Agile team in each cycle

Team

Profile	Functions
- Cross-functional and multi-disciplinary - Specialists and experts in their job - Focused on delivery - Skilled communicators - Self-organized	- Their job is to deliver the tasks that have been agreed on with the Product Owner
	Responsible For...
	- Delivering the tasks from the Product Backlog - Bringing updates on progress to the Daily Meeting - Testing the product or work developed - Raising issues that prevent the team from moving forward to the Product Owner and Scrum Master - Talking to each other

Tools[5]:

- The **Product Backlog** is, without a doubt, the main document of this methodology. It states all the tasks in the team's scope and it is a living document that will allow us to select and prioritize tasks for each Sprint, or cycle. The Product Backlog is maintained by the Product Owner.

- The **Kanban tool** is the board that will allow every single person in the team to see the status of each task in the cycle. The Kanban board is updated by each team member with the updated status of each task and

[5] Source: *Scrum Alliance, https://www.scrumalliance.org/*

is public to all the team members, including the Scrum Master and the Product Owner.

- The **planning template** will allow the team to put together the tasks and capacity for each Sprint in the planning meeting. The planning template is maintained by the Scrum Master in collaboration with the whole team.

In the next chapter, we will deep dive into each one of these tools and share potential structures that could help increase the productivity of the team.

Meetings[6]:

Meeting	When	Goal
Sprint Planning	Before each cycle or Sprint. It sets the beginning of the cycle	The goal is to align the goal of the Sprint, tasks that will be delivered during the cycle or Sprint, and their priorities.
Daily Meeting	Every day inside the cycle, besides the last day of the cycle	The goal is for the team to share updates on the Sprint evolution.
Refinement Meeting	When 60% of the length of the cycle has been consumed	The goal is to review and update the product backlog and re-assess any estimation on current user stories.
Sprint Review	End of the cycle	The goal is to go through all tasks in the scope of the Sprint and their output, it is an inspection meeting where the Product Owner also provides feedback about each task.
Sprint Retrospective	End of the cycle	The goal is to discuss openly anything related to how the team works together as a whole. It will help to develop an action plan and improve the way the team executes further Sprints.

In the next chapter, we will better understand the rationale behind these meetings and how to make them as productive as possible.

---

[6] Source: *Scrum Alliance, https://www.scrumalliance.org/*

THE PLAYBOOK

Now that we understand the principles and the artifacts of Agile Methodologies it is time to bring these concepts to real life situations. In this chapter, we are going to talk about what it's like to be running projects under this methodology and what practices can be useful to ensure great outcomes and maximize the success of our teams. Additionally, we will also present materials that you could easily use for your teams, and powerful knowledge that I have learnt through experience and that can be easily adapted to fit our framework. The first steps will be necessary to kick-off the project, but the rest are iterative steps that repeat themselves on each cycle or Sprint. If you have experience in Agile Methodologies you can skip ahead to the next chapter! If not, this can be a quick guide to start implementing this methodology.

Step 1. Defining high-level goals (one-off)

Let's start by asking ourselves, what do we want to achieve with this methodology? We want to achieve our goals and make progress in a valuable manner, either professionally or personally. Clear, right? We need to start by understanding what our goals are. This is a crucial part regardless of the nature of our goals. From a corporate perspective ,a high-level goal could be "Increase the quality of the service we provide to our customers" or "Increase the number of services we provide to our internal clients" and, from a personal perspective, it could be something like "Develop and improve my professional branding inside my industry," or even "Complete a Marathon." They can be broader or more concrete but, since they are high-level goals, I would always keep it as broad as possible for this initial step.

For your personal affairs, this is a reflection you need to make by having a strong sense of self-awareness. You need to understand what would make you improve but also what makes you feel happy and satisfied if you are spending a lot of time achieving these goals. Don't forget these goals will determine what you are spending your time on.

From a professional perspective, defining high-level goals is probably one of the most important exercises you need to make as a leader; being able to align with your stakeholders and making sure these goals are aligned to the company's goals is necessary. Are these goals written in stone? I would say no, they are not. It is convenient to allow some flexibility in order to adapt your team to the direction of the company, having said this when defining, have the following in consideration:

- these goals will define what you and your team spend time on, making sure they are consistent and coherent is worthwhile
- if you change your high-level goals frequently this will result in your team losing focus, lacking direction, and getting dispersed
- use your good sense to judge:
    - reviewing high-level goals every 6 months is not bad at all, even if it results in small changes or adding or removing goals
    - changing high-level goals every 2 months, can jeopardize the rest of the goals and the team's wellbeing

Let me show you an example of what a simple high-level goal could look like:

Goal	Success	Projects
Increase my social network presence	Increase number of likes and organic followers by 10%	Social - User acquisition
		Social – Engagement
Achieve sustainable financial habits	Increase the amount of money saved per annum by 30%	Financial – Increase Income
		Financial – Spending management

Step 2. Define team and relevant stakeholders (one-off)

The next important thing is to start putting faces to the people involved in our methodology, after this step you should be able to answer with a name or a set of names (or department name) for the following roles:

- Scrum Master (1 person)
- Product Owner (ideally 1 person)
- Team (>1 person, best practices recommend Agile teams within a size between 3-9 members)
- Key stakeholders, as long as…
  - they are impacted by our work
  - they are sources of information for our work
  - they are clients or the customer we provide service to
  - they need to be informed about our work

Step 3. Create the Product Backlog (one-off)

The Product Backlog is the most important document, it is maintained by the Product Owner and my advice is that you keep it as straightforward as possible. The Product Backlog carries the following information:

- information about the tasks
- information about the stakeholders
- information about the projects
- relevant information to define the outcomes of each task

Let's see an example,

ID of Task	Topic or Project	As the Product Owner I want to...	so that...	and I will consider the task as done when...	Priority	Status	Stakeholder(s)
001	Social – Engagement	create two initial posts in Instagram related to Indian Cuisine	I can test the engagement we are generating right now	I see two new posts with pictures and hashtags and a nice caption	Medium	Not Started	Client 1
002	Financial – Increase Income	gather a list of the 5 best performing investment funds from the last 3 years	I can shortlist a reliable security to start investing some money	we see a table of investment funds with relevant performance and risk information	High	On Going	Internal Stakeholder 1
004	Financial – Spending management	develop a list of all our fixed monthly costs	we can assess which expenses are unnecessary	we are able to determine the amount, relevance and frequency of all our payments to third parties	Medium	Delayed	Internal Stakeholder 1
006	Financial – Spending management	contact the suppliers of our top 2 costs to schedule a meeting to renegotiate	we are set the grounds to reduce our costs	negotiation meetings are scheduled	High	Blocked	Internal Stakeholder 1

This document needs to be maintained, so my advice is to keep it as clean as possible and reduce the number of people that can modify it. Being able to set a public non-editable version could help out the team and stakeholders. My second piece of advice is to be open-minded about the structure; if you feel that adding another attribute or column to the table would bring considerable clarity or value to the team, feel free to do it, and last but not least, make a non-editable version public, this will provide a lot of transparency to the team and stakeholders.

Step 4. Planning meeting (iterative, triggers the Sprint)

The planning meeting is the initial step of the Sprint cycle, is conducted by the Scrum Master and the Product Owner, and the whole team participates. The goal of the meeting is to define the length and the goal of the Sprint (what we want to achieve in this next cycle) and align and estimate the effort of each task that the team will work on during the Sprint. The duration of this meeting can be adapted to the capacity of the team (the bigger the team is, the more tasks are discussed in the meeting), but we should prefer as short as possible, between 30 and 60 minutes should be enough.

In this meeting, the Product Owner will explain what he or she wants to achieve in this Sprint (or cycle), the team will start discussing the tasks in the product backlog that are going to be tackled, and discussing how much effort (in time or days) it would take to get them done. It is also important in this meeting to forecast any impact that the team, as experts, can foresee, like potential roadblocks or investigations that need to be made in order to mitigate any risk and achieve the best result possible.

First, we need to decide the length of the Sprint, it is recommended to use between 2 and 4 week cycles, and before deciding I would have in consideration the following (among others):

- capacity of the team; when there is a higher availability of the team, shorter Sprints are more effective if part of the team is unavailable or on vacation, a longer Sprint can be more effective
- alignment between stakeholders; if the Product Owner feels that he or she will need to align with stakeholders in order to deliver the user stories it may help add more time to the Sprint (and therefore more

tasks, since the capacity increases) to reduce the risk of team members being idle

What is important is that the length can be changed from Sprint to another. The goal is to provide the necessary length to the Sprint that allows effective work to be achieved by maximizing the time that the team is able to work in the user stories without roadblocks, reducing idle time, or dependencies.

Second, we need to align the capacity of the team. Imagine we have agreed to do a 2 week Sprint (can be between 2 and 4), and our team has 5 members, assuming our workdays are 5 per week, our capacity is WORKDAYS x MEMBERS (in days) or WORKING HOURS x MEMBERS (in hours).

Let's see an example:

A team of 5 members, working 8 hours per day, 5 days per week for two weeks would have a capacity of 50 days, or 400 hours.

Now that we know the capacity, we want to start the assessment on how much time or capacity each task consumes, this will be a discussion where each team member will vote an estimation ("I think this task will take 4 days") and explain the rationale behind that time. The Product Owner will start explaining the details of the task and want needs to be achieved, and then each team member will vote (simultaneously).

Now, as leaders we need to encourage the team to be as diligent as possible,

- it would help if the Product Owner shared these tasks beforehand (making the product backlog public) so that the team can have time to go through the tasks before the meeting and have as much information as possible about how much time it will actually take to do something and investigate any impact,
- it also helps to generate a feeling of self-accountability so that each team member understands that estimating correctly will help increase the team trust and expectation management both with stakeholders and the Product Owner.

As team members what do we need to have in consideration before estimating the time effort of a task?

- Any analysis that needs to be done beforehand and that can delay the task
- Any dependencies on other teams that need to be untangled
- The complexity of the task and the risk of not having reliable sources of information on time
- Understanding clearly what the Product Owner wants to see and in which format
- Understanding the impact of these tasks in any other teams or current processes (or systems)

When team members are voting, each one of them will have their own estimation. Sometimes they might be aligned and other times there will be outliers. The important thing is to discuss as a team the implications of the task in order to reach a consensus. It's important to encourage the team to ask any questions to the Product Owner so that everybody has a clear perception on what is expected for each task.

An example on how this planning might look[7] (top-down priority):

Sprint Goal: put in place an initial financial planning draft			
Sprint End-Date: 15/04/2018			
		Capacity	50 days
Task ID	Task Name (User Story)	Team Estimation	Capacity Left
002	gather a list of the 5 best performing investment funds from the last 3 years	2 days	48 days
004	develop a list of all our fixed monthly costs	2 days	46 days
006	contact the suppliers of our top 2 costs to schedule a meeting to renegotiate	1 day	45 days
...	...	...	...
00X	xxxxx	xxxxx	-2 days

This exercise would need to be done for the number of tasks necessary to leave the last column "Capacity Left" in 0 or near to zero negative (we want to add extra tasks in case there is time for them).

Step 5. Daily meetings (iterative)

---

[7] Source: *Smartsheet, https://www.smartsheet.com/*

The Daily Meeting is, in my opinion, one of the most effective meetings a professional can have, it is a daily 10 to 15-minute meeting where the Product Owner and Team talk about the evolution of the Sprint and it has a very simple structure that needs to be followed. In this meeting each team member answers the following questions about the tasks or user stories agreed to in the planning meeting.

- What did I do yesterday?
- What will I spend my time doing today?
- What is blocking me from completing this task on time?

How can we make these meetings even more effective?

- I would keep the Scrum Master in these meetings, it will help to have somebody that reinforces the methodology for when people go off script and keep on talking. Keeping the meeting straight to the point is really important.
- Conduct the meeting standing up, believe me, it makes a difference. When people sit down and start talking, it's really difficult to stop them. You want to keep the meeting as effective as possible. Less is more.
- Encourage people to speak up about the third question, it's the most important one.
- Allow the Product Owner to intervene at the end of the meeting to provide...
  - o business insights that he or she thinks the team might need in order to get the task done
  - o changes in priority in case something new has become a priority
  - o relevant updates from meetings with stakeholders that do have an impact on the team's work

Step 6. Refinement meeting (iterative)

The Refinement Meeting, also known as backlog refinement, is a recurrent 30-60 minute meeting held by the Product Owner and either part or all of the Team. During this meeting, the backlog is reviewed, ensuring that it contains updated information about the time estimates for each tasks, that tasks are aligned with current priorities, and that the product backlog is updated with any recent discovered information or new requests.

What type of changes might you end up making in the Refinement meeting? (source agilealliance.org)

- Remove user stories that are not relevant anymore
- Creating user stories based on newly discovered needs
- Re-assessing the priority of existing user stories
- Correcting estimates of user stories

Besides the backlog refinement, a common use of this meeting is to manage expectations looking forward to the Sprint Review. It can be used to go through the tasks or user stories that have been allocated to that Sprint and align on which tasks are going to be completed and which ones might get delayed.

Step 7. Sprint Review (iterative, closes the Sprint)

The Sprint Review is a recurrent 30-60 minute meeting, held at the end of the Sprint, where stakeholders, the Product Owner, and the team go through the user stories that have been developed during this period. The goal is to inspect the tasks and to discuss what issues the team ran into during the Sprint, confirm if the task achieves the status of "Done", and agree with stakeholders about the next steps.

A potential storyline to handle this meeting is for each User Story to talk about:

- The goal of the User Story
- What problems did the team run into
- What has been the outcome of the User Story
- Inspect the result or piece of work or see an example

It is encouraged to bring impacted stakeholders or internal clients to these meetings if they are impacted by our work. That way the team can gather feedback if needed and the communication flows effectively across the organization. It is also a great way to validate on the spot the work that has been done.

Step 8. Sprint Retrospective (iterative)

The Sprint Retrospective is a recurrent 30-60 minute meeting, held at the end of the Sprint, where Scrum Master, Product Owner and the team go through a discussion about the way the team worked in the Sprint, what worked well, what could be improved and what actions the team and the Scrum Master need to take in order to improve. This meeting is really important to bring self-awareness to the team in what aspects need to be improved for the next Sprint.

BALANCING DONE VS PERFECT

How to balance perfect and done? How to make sure things reach a marketable level of quality without jeopardizing the roll-out? Perfectionism can destroy your will to push these projects forward and make you procrastinate in things that won't add value to your goals, whereas lack of quality can destroy your entire project's outcome or your reputation, you want to find a balance that allows you to market something with a decent level of quality whilst being very proactive when searching for issues and gathering feedback from users and stakeholders.

Think about the business value

Example 1. Imagine you need to build an eCommerce website, and you have thirty days to market this website, you need to build the prototype, add products, build workflows, payment system, etc. Now imagine you have a spelling mistake in a description, how much of an issue do you think it will be to your business? In this case perfectionism will distract you from what is important which is testing the eCommerce website and making sure people follow through the conversion funnel you have designed. Now, imagine you have a spelling mistake in the Data Protection Policy, or in the Bank account information, that spelling mistake might have an impact in your business, it might be a liability.

So, the question is, what delivers business value or what can be a liability, that needs to be perfected. If not, focus on what is important.

Example 2. Imagine this spelling mistake is not in a long description inside the product page of one of your products as mentioned above, but in the description of an Instagram post, in this second case the spelling mistake might be so evident that it might shift attention from the whole post to the spelling mistake, that has a business impact, therefore it is important.

Manage perfection through the scope

Perfectionism might kill your ability to prioritize, might shift your attention to lower value tasks rather than focusing in what brings value, I have seen people so worried with the position of a textbox in a presentation that they were forgetting to double check the content. When you are defining tasks, you need to make sure you scope them with a perfectionism mindset, and by that, I mean, flawless, precise, but smartly scoped to what brings actual value.

Example 1. Imagine you are building an App, and you want to publish it as soon as possible, but you know is far from perfect, ask yourself which features are people going to focus on, for instance if the app is related to sharing dining experiences, anything that is user public information or sharing features should work perfectly, make sure the scope of the User Story includes a clear scope to ensure things are going to be tested. Instead, something like a specific field from the venue's profile that won't be shared might not be worth your attention so make sure the User Story's definition has that in consideration.

Your User Stories must be oriented to bring immediate value, make sure these user stories are defined in a way that when your market this feature everything goes smoothly, but also make sure that the scope of the User Story focuses on what is important. The best way to know this is asking yourself if someone (and how many more) has explicitly asked for this feature or what is the cost of opportunity of not marketing this feature as soon as possible.

Build the pressure that will make you iterate to improve the product

If I had waited for this book to be perfect I wouldn't have published it in my entire life, waiting for something to be perfect before putting it out there is a waste of time, instead you want to prepare a viable product and put it out there so that you start feeling immediately the pressure to improve it, but you need to follow through. Stop thinking it's going to be perfect or that nobody is going to complain about it, you are going to get negative feedback, there are going to be issues during the roll-out and you must be prepared to quick turnarounds and damage control. Gather the feedback, structure it, rationalize it and then act as soon as possible to fix it. Once you are in the game, it will be extremely difficult to stop, the pressure around you will make you want to improve it, doing this a million times will result in having something near to perfection.

Things might not need to be perfect, but they need to be precise

These are concepts that are easy to mix up, precise means it's accurate, exact, and perfection is related to the level of completeness or the fact that no more requisites are needed. Even if you don't need your product to be perfect you do want to make sure your product, whatever it is, it is precise, accurate, dependable and reliable. That it serves its purpose.

Let's take for example an analytical dashboard, perfection would mean that the dashboard doesn't need more variables or that every measurable item is included, whereas precision means the information contained for the variables included is accurate and trustworthy. It is way better to start with less variables and make sure they are precise end-to-end, reliable and trustworthy than try to have a fancy big dashboard with all sorts of variables that might not be as impactful as you think, prioritizing preciseness over completeness will allow you to focus on key metrics.

Stakeholders matter

Perfection is important in some cases; imagine you are rolling out a product for demanding customers or end-users, you need to make sure that everything you market is as near to perfect as possible, also you want to make sure any feature that is related to the customer journey or the customer's financial experience is as polished as possible.

 Now imagine this feature is being rolled out for an internal client (another department within your company), you should understand beforehand the sensitiveness of the issue, and the impact in this department. You might need to work closely with this department to reduce the scope in order to achieve a near to perfection experience, despite what you decide you definitely will have to manage expectations and align upfront with what they can expect to receive, despite it not being perfect.

Rationalize your priorities

With all the above let's try to rationalize how to balance done versus perfect. The steps are the following:

1. Gather a list of User Stories of everything you need to do, these User Stories are unrefined User Stories
2. Evaluate User Stories on merit based on three variables:
    a. Direct business impact
    b. Liability or blocking issue
    c. Sensitive impact on stakeholder
3. Based on these three variables order your tasks from higher to lower
4. Start polishing the definition of the User Story to make sure the following happens:
    a. You deliver the main feature correctly
    b. You reduce any corner case that might affect the quality
    c. You define very well what needs to be tested and the definition of success
    d. Roll-out steps and damage control are defined and followed

COFFEE BREAK!

Hey there!

I wanted to take this opportunity to thank you for buying this book, since it will help extend a methodology that is value-driven, focused on results, on people and on delivering to your eco-system. As a gift I want to provide you with the templates that you can use to start building this methodology and get it running!

Scan here to access all the templates, you just need to make a copy to your own drive and read the guidelines carefully, hope you find it useful. As usual in Agile, feedback is super welcome!

AGILE LIFE I. HIGH LEVEL GOALS AND PROJECTS

Now that we have been able to understand the principles and mechanisms of this methodology it is time to start the experiment! I would recommend that regardless the industry in which you work in to do this experiment for yourself, and once you have tested it apply it to your teams. It will take time, you won't get it right at first but eventually you will see how the team starts gaining momentum and working more aligned. It might also help for you to hire a Scrum Master. For more information feel free to reach out, I have added contact details at the end of this book.

Which initiatives do you wish to start in your life? Setting high level goals is probably one of the most exciting parts of this experiment, this part is pretty strategic. When you are defining these goals you need to think in medium term. They need to be broad enough so that you can fit a few short term initiatives that will help achieve that goal. You need to make sure you deeply understand where do you want to see yourself in one or two years. Think about goals that also generate meaningful impact in your life, and if it is possible, those that will generate a strong feeling of achievement. High level goals need to represent things in which you are willing and excited to spend time on. There is no point on choosing a goal that is going to make you feel frustrated.

Let's see an example. of how to define these goals. Remember we need to define them in a broad way and based on that we will decide which projects and initiative we will include in our product backlog.

Goal examples:

"Achieve major progression in my health and sports habits",
"Put in place an ambitious financial plan that will serve my financial goals",
"Achieve substantial improvements in my professional relations"

---

or even "Make 2021 a great year"

Value vs Results

One of the main goals of this book is to show the benefits of this methodology regardless of the nature of our projects. For that we need to understand when we need to set goals that generate value and when to set goals that help us achieve tangible and material goals. For instance, it is way different if you work for a sales team, where you most likely will have a preference for tangible results versus when you are setting personal goals where generating value will be a legitimate outcome.

Let's see an example of a goal that is focused on results versus a goal that is focused on generating value:

"Increase overall sales by 30%" – simple, this one is focused on results, it is really easy to measure, and the goal is clear.

"Improve my professional relations" – this one is as legitimate as the previous one, but is not result oriented, you won't be able to measure it, or at least in a reliable manner. It is not something that will materialize or be tangible in an explicit way. Despite all this it will definitely generate some value to you as a professional.

Defining Goals

Before defining my goals I decided to think about what big topics I wanted to improve and handle them as an Agile project, I started by identifying areas in which I wanted to succeed and achieve better results, but also areas that were difficult to spend time on because I usually got carried away by my daily routine. The first had to do with financial goals, I have realized that even though I work in a thriving industry, it is subject to such rapid change that sometimes it destabilizes you. Also the fact that we assume higher risks than other generations. Sometimes I have felt it would be smart to have different and diverse streams of income to build a stronger financial position and always be prepared for turnarounds.

The second had to do with professional networks. I had felt that at my age and with my name (a name that is pretty uncommon in Spain), I needed to start working on my branding and professional connections so that I could be perceived as a strong contributor to the community. I wanted not only to improve my personal reputation, but also extend my connections as much as possible as a way to improve my employability and branding as an industry known leader. But this takes time and effort so Agile Methodologies would help me set up the bases.

See examples of one of each, a goal that is focused on results and another that adds value:

High-level goals
Set in place a financial structure that allows me to thrive financially in medium and long term
Drive professional initiatives to boost my network

For this experiment we will focus on those that add substantial value to my career. I am going to start defining the initiatives and thus the project names I want to use during execution:

High-level goals	Initiatives
Drive professional initiatives to boost my network	Start contributing to my network in areas I have extensive experience on
Drive professional initiatives to boost my network	Add new skills by leveraging on-line education platforms
Drive professional initiatives to boost my network	Launch and roll-out professional side projects that will help me acquire applicable experience to my industry

Now that we have detailed our initiatives let's set appealing names to the projects. I know a fancy name doesn't change anything, but I really think it helps to build motivation around the project.

High-level goals	Project Names
Drive professional initiatives to	Industry Contributions

boost my network	
Drive professional initiatives to boost my network	Upskilling
Drive professional initiatives to boost my network	Entrepreneurship

What's next? Sprint I, we will define the length, capacity, and planning for the first two weeks.

CASE III. MAKE IT HARD TO STOP RATHER THAN HARD TO START

I was having a slice of pizza at a well-known restaurant at Neal's Yard, I was sitting there with one of the owners of a startup in London I had invested in and wanted to know more about what pain points the owners were running into when executing projects with a very limited budget. My goal was to understand how Agile Methodologies could help them in better execution, with a constrained budget and a unstructured team, whilst achieving their goals. They have already raised some funds from small investors and they weren't in a position to substantially increase their budget via fundraising in order to bring in senior professionals to execute projects, but without seniority they felt these initiatives were becoming too big to handle. Even before handling, they were becoming too big to structure which meant team members had a hard time understanding where to start and how to follow when something got blocked. They weren't able to dedicate time to support their teams and therefore the lack of guidance was affecting the timelines.

I started asking about these big projects and how big they were. After all, it was a very small startup. The problem wasn't the projects being too big, but that the team lacked the guidance on how to break the problem into smaller pieces and how to prioritize these pieces in order to start gaining momentum. This was due to the lack of experience in these kind of projects combined with a very busy management. I had seen this before, whenever I had seen the lack of guidance there was a risk of team members procrastinating to no fault of their own. A risk of problems not being structured with a growth mentality where bigger problems are located at the beginning, impeding the team to gain momentum. I then knew that one of my main goals in this book was to leverage this methodology to reduce procrastination, to help ourselves to order problems in a sequence that goes from low effort to high effort so that it becomes easier to start than to stop. When you have gained momentum and

---

you are in it 100%, it is way more difficult to leave things incomplete. This is also one of the roles a Scrum Master should assume beyond its traditional role, guiding the Product Owner in structuring the User Stories so that the team gains momentum quickly and the stories are easy to digest and complete, this way we will improve the way our people come to work.

How do you make it harder to stop than to start?

- Assess Effort
- Assess Impact/Importance
- Assess Dependencies
- Assess Impact on Stakeholder Relations
- Assess Urgency

Using a point system and a matrixial approach we should be able to order the tasks from high priority to low priority, depending on the sum, but also based on the matrix evaluation, we will know what the immediate next step is. Ordering them from high to low will allow you to get a snapshot on your priorities. Since this is not scientific, once you have been able to draft an initial approach you should feel free to promote or demote any task beyond their grade. This will only provide an initial structure subject to minor modifications. Your gut is also an important variable, it is just one I cannot measure here.

Start by making a non-scientific assessment on these. You just need to rank them as high or low and then use these matrixes and their scoring system, to not only prioritize, but to take action.

Matrix 1: Effort-Impact

	Low Effort	High Effort
Low Impact/Importance	2	1

High Impact/Importance	4	2

Based on this Matrix, here's what kind of actions you can take:

- If a task is Low Impact and High Effort, you might want to break it into smaller pieces and check if any of those pieces can be deprioritized.
- If a task is Low Impact and Low Effort, you should evaluate if you can remove the task from the Product Backlog or slip at the end/bottom of a Sprint Plan but with less priority.
- If a task is High Impact and High Effort, you should break it into smaller pieces and evaluate different team members whose combined skills could allow to share the effort of these tasks.
- If a task is High Impact and Low Effort, just go for it!

Matrix 2: Dependency and Stakeholder Impact

	Low Dependency	High Dependency
Low Impact on SH	2	1
High Impact on SH	4	2

Based on this Matrix what kind of actions you can take:

- If a task is Low Impact on SH and High Dependency, you should push it backwards in the Sprint Planning[8] or even in the Product Backlog, depending on other variables like the overall impact and the impact on stakeholders.

---

[8] Source: *Scrum Alliance, https://www.scrumalliance.org/*

- If a task is Low Impact on SH and Low Dependency, based on the overall impact you could move it forward or backward, since there is no dependency, it allows the team to work on it.
- If a task is High Impact on SH and High Dependency, as Scrum Master you need to push for the necessary meetings to happen as soon as possible, guide the Product Owner on who to reach out to and how to structure the meeting so that the team obtains what is needed on time. This is a Servant Leadership approach, which is becoming a crucial skill for leaders nowadays.
- If a task is High Impact on SH and Low Dependency, go for it. There is nothing stopping you and it helps the brand of the team to collaborate with other stakeholders and allows the team to feel valued.

Matrix 3: Impact and Urgency

	Low Urgency	High Urgency
Low Impact/Importance	1	2
High Impact/Importance	2	4

This matrix serves as another scoring variable, it will help determine the overall scoring of the three but there are no actionable items beside assessing the impact and urgency of the tasks to get a score.

With all the above plus the actions generated by each matrix you should feel comfortable in playing around with tasks so that an effective configuration of User Stories allows your team to gain momentum and speed up the Sprint, making it hard to procrastinate and easy to move forward. The same way you are kind to your team, you should be kind to yourself. Do this in a personal project that you have been procrastinating for a while. Break it into smaller pieces, allocate a few hours per week, and create a smart configuration of tasks starting with those that require less effort and do have some impact. You might find out that you were procrastinating because of the structure and magnitude of the problems and not because you were being lazy. The Scrum Master can use this as a guide to take action whenever it feels right based on these guidelines. One of the main responsibilities of a Scrum Master is to remove any impediments that the team has but, by using this approach, not only we are removing impediments but also dynamizing our relationship between the Team, Product Owner and stakeholders.

SPRINT I

Now that we have been able to understand the principles and artifacts of this methodology, it is time to start applying it to those initiatives we have chosen. Let's start with the planning!

Sprint I – Planning

What should be the goal for this initial Sprint? Let's go back to our table of projects.

High-level goals	Project Names
Drive professional initiatives to boost my network	Industry Contributions
Drive professional initiatives to boost my network	Upskilling
Drive professional initiatives to boost my network	Entrepreneurship

Since we are starting these projects from scratch, I feel the initial Sprint should be all about research, understanding each topic better, and gathering information from the internet that will help us better understand what next steps we need to include in our Product Backlog for each topic. For instance, for the first project, "Industry Contributions", I might want to explore which ways I can start contributing to my industry and then set an action plan to start building a brand.

Sprint Goal: Perform necessary research to prepare action plans			
Sprint End-Date:			
		Capacity	
Task ID	Task Name (User Story)	Team Estimation	Capacity Left

Now that we have clearly stated our goal, which needs to be simple and explicit, it is time to decide the length of the Sprint. The length of the Sprint can range from 2 to 4 weeks. Since I want to start with quick cycles and put my projects in place as quickly as possible, I don't have much dependency, and I don't have many stakeholders to align with for this initial cycle, I am choosing a Sprint of 2 weeks. I have always had the feeling that people push harder when due dates arrive, so by keeping the cycles short I might generate a sense of having a deadline without this being one. All the above means that from the planning meeting to the Sprint Review meeting we will have around 10 working days (I am allowing myself weekends off). Imagine we started Friday, the 1st of November, I would allow myself to work until Friday, the 15th of November.

Sprint Goal: Perform necessary research to prepare action plans			
Sprint End-Date: 15/11			
		Capacity	
Task ID	Task Name (User Story)	Team Estimation	Capacity Left

Once the length of the Sprint is defined, I need to decide how much time I want to dedicate, that is known as Capacity. Since I am employed and I want to also save time to rest and do sports, I am allocating just 1 hour per day for these projects, it should be enough for this initial Sprint. If I were to assign a higher capacity at the beginning, I would risk not having enough time since during workdays there is too much hustle. I want to test my ability to dedicate 5 hours per week to these tasks and if necessary increase this amount in the future. There is nothing wrong about adjusting the capacity on each Sprint. When we have Agile teams, it's normal that capacities vary due to people going on vacations, appointments, or team members having to dedicate time to other stuff. In each planning we should ask the team their capacity for the next few weeks so that we can precisely estimate the number of hours we have available.

Sprint Goal: Perform necessary research to prepare action plans			
Sprint End-Date: 15/11			
		Capacity (in hours)	10 (1hrs x 10 days)
Task ID	Task Name (User Story)	Team Estimation	Capacity Left

In this experiment, I am going to act as Scrum Master, Product Owner and Team, but in practice these should always be separate roles, so keep that in mind when trying to apply this methodology to your team. The Product Owner should have the details of the tasks and once explained the team would estimate the time needed to complete the task as per the definition of done[9]

---

[9] Source: *Scrum Alliance, https://www.scrumalliance.org/*

made by the Product Owner. Once defined, ideally the team would then start estimating each task, the team should outline the details, discuss the scope, and reach consensus on the estimation. In this case, the estimation will be done just by me, which is not ideal, since there is no one else to challenge me, but for this experiment we will have to go with what we have.

The first task I would like to add is related to the project Industry Contributions, it has to be simple for this first Sprint, I am thinking about just focusing on research, let's see how this task would look in my product backlog:

ID of Task	Topic or Project	As the Product Owner I want to...	so that...	and I will consider the task as done when...	Priority	Status	Stakeholder(s)
001	Industry Contributions	draft an initial list on ways I can contribute to my industry	I can shortlist a few to start working on	I receive a list of ways to contribute with details such as effort and impact	Medium	Not Started	Product Owner

The Product Owner has to explain the context of this task, any potential dependencies, any corner cases the team needs to have in consideration, and what he or she expects to see as an outcome. This straight to the point explanation can help the team on completing tasks successfully and reducing any risks of expectation mismatch at the Sprint Review. The team on the other side has to estimate the task based on this information, and realistically speaking, based on their experience, what analysis they need to make, if there is any briefing on this task needed, if there are any dependencies the task carries, impact on other tasks or processes, all combined to formulate a solid estimation. In order to achieve this, it is always convenient that prospective user stories are shared beforehand with the team so that they can arrive to the planning meeting with more context and make the most out of the estimation process.

In this case, the task is simple, there is no dependency and no impact on other tasks, I can gather the information on my own from the internet and I have a clear view on what outcome the Product Owner expects. My estimation is that gathering all the information, structuring the data, and filling in the details that the Product Owner has specified would take around 3 hours (not necessarily in one sitting).

After repeating this same process until my capacity would turn negative, I got the following:

Sprint Goal: Perform necessary research to prepare action plans			
Sprint End-Date: 15/11			
		Capacity (in hours)	10 (1hrs x 10 days)
Task ID	Task Name (User Story)	Team Estimation	Capacity Left
001	draft an initial list on ways I can contribute to my industry	3	7
002	draft an initial list on courses I could leverage for my professional career	3	4
003	draft an initial list on initiatives I would love to launch	3	1
004	gather different channels or networks through which I can contribute	2	-1

This is how my planning would look after adding all the tasks I feel I need to undertake this Sprint. It is convenient to add a few more tasks once you have reached the 0 hours of capacity left. The goal of doing this is to make sure that if there is any time left we have something to work on until the end of the Sprint. Let's see how the Product Backlog would look:

ID of Task	Topic or Project	As the Product Owner I want to...	so that...	and I will consider the task as done when...	Priority	Status	Stakeholder(s)
001	Industry Contributions	draft an initial list on ways I can contribute to my industry	I can shortlist a few to start working on	I receive a list of ways to contribute with details such as effort and impact	High	Not Started	Product Owner
002	Upskilling	draft an initial list on courses I could leverage for my professional career	I can shortlist a few to start taking them	I receive a list of courses with details such as topic, effort and level of difficulty	Medium	Not Started	Product Owner
003	Entrepreneurship	draft an initial list on initiatives I would love to launch	I can shortlist a few topics to start working on	I receive a list of topics with details such as impact, effort and investment needed	High	Not Started	Product Owner
004	Industry Contributions	gather different channels or networks through which I can contribute	I can prepare the action plan according to these channels	I receive a list of channels that I will use to contribute	Medium	Not Started	Product Owner

Imagine I decided that some of these would have a higher priority than others, we could change not only the Priority in the Product Backlog but also their order in the planning table. For instance, imagine Entrepreneurship is not as urgent for me as Industry Contributions but more urgent than Upskilling. I could change the priority in the product backlog of Entrepreneurship and separately reorganize tasks related to this topic to tackle them first. The key takeaway is that the methodology should serve us, not limit us. In this case I have decided to bump Entrepreneurship User Stories in this Sprint, leaving the Sprint planning as follows:

Sprint Goal: Perform necessary research to prepare action plans			
Sprint End-Date: 15/11			
		Capacity (in hours)	10 (1hrs x 10 days)
Task ID	Task Name (User Story)	Team Estimation	Capacity Left
001	draft an initial list on ways I can contribute to my industry	3	7
003	**draft an initial list on initiatives I would love to launch**	**3**	**4**
002	draft an initial list on courses I could leverage for my professional career	3	1
004	gather different channels or networks through which I can contribute	2	-1

Once the planning is done, the team can start executing these User Stories. Since we have agreed the capacity is 1 hour per day, we should expect that commitment from the team members, in this case just me. Somebody could think that these tasks seem too simple, too easy going, but as we have seen before we need to make it easy to start at the beginning. That is achieved by setting the bar to a level that makes us feel we are moving forward and being able to set the bar higher on each Sprint moving forward. Still, if you feel that the bar is set too low for you, you can add a little bit more complexity to these tasks, for instance "draft initial list of ways I can contribute to my industry based on the current trends and with new approaches".

Sprint I – Daily Meetings

The Daily Meetings will allow the team to keep the Product Owner posted about the progress of the Sprint. At the beginning I would recommend looping in the Scrum Master, since the team might need help in structuring these meetings. The goal of the meeting is to provide a clear update to the Product

Owner and to make everybody aware of any roadblocks that can stop the team from moving forward.

The storyline follows this pattern:
- What did I do yesterday?
- What will I spend my time on today?
- What is blocking me from completing this task on time?

An example for the first Daily Meeting could be:
- What did I do yesterday? *Yesterday I started drafting the initial list of ways I can contribute to my industry.*
- What will I spend my time on today? *Today, I will start gathering details, such as time, effort, and impact in order to correctly rank them.*
- What is blocking me from completing this task on time? *Some details can be difficult to foresee before actually starting to develop these projects. Also, I would like to know if we want to include financial contributions or only professional contributions.*

At this point, it is clear that to move forward with the task the Product Owner and the person in charge of pushing this task forward need to connect. They could align next steps in the same Daily Meeting if it is quick, but I would recommend always moving to an offline conversation after the Daily is done, this way we keep the daily focused on updates. Remember, the Daily Meeting should never exceed 15 minutes, so it is crucial to coach the team to provide straight to the point updates. It is important also to generate a good judgment on the level of granularity we wish to provide about the tasks. This depends on factors such as the complexity of the task, the technical details and how easy it would be for the Product Owner to understand, the goal of the Sprint, and others.

Providing updates at the Daily Meeting with more granularity could look like:

- What did I do yesterday? *Yesterday I started drafting the initial list of ways I can contribute to my industry, having separated these between ones that may have an immediate impact versus those that are a long-term value proposal.*

This same meeting will take place every day of the Sprint except for the last day, when the Sprint Review will mark the end of the Sprint. Even though the

Daily Meeting is a short meeting it is probably one of the most important meetings to keep the methodology alive and useful. At any Daily Meeting the Product Owner can ask the team to share beforehand the work done for some User Stories, just to start providing feedback or to start planning the next Sprint. In this case we want to see the list before the Refinement Meeting so that we can start adding new tasks to our Product Backlog.

In the next chapter we will provide some tips to maximize the productivity of these meetings that have been gathered through experience. The goal is to always make the meeting as short and effective as possible whilst keeping everybody in the room aligned.

Sprint I – Refinement Meeting

The Refinement Meeting usually takes place a few days before the Sprint review, it usually takes between 30 and 60 minutes and the attendees are the Team, Product Owner, and Scrum Master. This meeting is a great moment not only to go through the User Stories due to the end of the Sprint, but also to manage the expectations of the Product Owner before the Sprint Review, allowing the Product Owner to quickly anticipate to stakeholders on any deviation or delay.

The Refinement Meeting in this Sprint will follow this agenda:

- We will go through the tasks that should be delivered by the end of the Sprint and realign expectations. We will also talk about any roadblocks that have stopped us from finishing or starting any of the tasks in our planning – 15 minutes
- The Product Owner will go through the tasks planned for the next Sprint so that the team can make the necessary due diligence to provide precise estimations on the planning meeting. – 15 minutes

The User Story will go through intends to provide a snapshot on the outcomes for each task at the date of the Sprint Review. The possible outcomes can be, "done", "blocked", "delayed", "not started", "not finished" or perhaps any of these with a comment. Needless to say, that the goal is always to have as many "done" as possible, keep the "not finished" to a minimum and ideally have a maximum of one or two "not started", more would mean that the Team is not estimating properly the efforts of each task. In this Sprint the result that we forecast has been the following:

Task ID	Task Name (User Story)	Status
001	draft an initial list on ways I can contribute to my industry	Done
003	draft an initial list of initiatives I would love to launch	Done
002	draft an initial list on courses I could leverage for my professional career	Done
004	gather different channels or networks through which I can contribute	Not Finished

Remember, we are providing a forecast on how the Sprint Review will look on the last day of the Sprint. Therefore one of the tasks that is marked as Done is probably not done as of the Refinement Meeting but we are confident it is going to be Done by the end of the Sprint. In this first Sprint, the scope was pretty easy, therefore there are no major deviations or surprises. Further we will see more examples where we need to reorganize tasks in order to ensure we maximize the ROI of the Sprint when some tasks are blocked.

Before moving to the next part of the Refinement Meeting, let's review the story line that we should hold on to depending on our outcome forecasts. Imagine you had a task that was blocked, ideally you should be able to answer the following questions; why is it blocked?, what can we complete from this task so that we tackle the blocked part by the next Sprint?, who could unblock it or which department we need to speak to if necessary? If it's a complication should more people of the team jump in and help? Even though each situation will be different and these questions are examples, and there is no obligation at all to prepare anything, in my experience having an answer to these questions can be really helpful to provide transparency and ability to the Scrum Master and Product Owner to help the team unblock issues.

These are the questions that I would advise you to be able to answer depending on each potential outcome case:

Status	Potential Questions
Blocked	Why is it blocked?
	What can we complete in regard to this task up until the Sprint Review?

	Who could help us unblock this task? Or which department?
	Is there any technical complication?
Delayed	What is the main cause for the delay?
	How much time will be needed?
	Is the delay due to something blocking us?
	Should the task be included in the next Sprint?
Not Finished	What will be missing?
	How much time will it take to complete it?
	Do you foresee any potential roadblocks to be taken in consideration?
	Should the task be included in the next Sprint?

For instance, Task ID 004, will not be finished by the end of this Sprint. An example on how could I explain the status of this task could be: *not finished, we will still be missing to assess the effort level required to get in some networks that require an admission process, it will probably take 2 more days (2 hours of capacity) to complete. Right now, the only potential roadblock I see is not being able to connect with people that can refer me on time. I would suggest we add this task to the next Sprint.*

The second part of the meeting aims to provide a snapshot on the next steps so that the team can make the necessary research in order to correctly estimate these tasks on the planning meeting. At this point, the Product Owner has already seen some of the work done during this Sprint. We can go through the priorities for the next Sprint and the different User Stories that we want to tackle in the short term. Even though we are trying to keep the team as updated as possible, small changes can be arranged in the priorities between the Refinement Meeting and the planning meeting.

ID of Task	Topic or Project	As the Product Owner I want to...	so that...	and I will consider the task as done when...	Priority	Status	Stakeholder(s)
005	Industry Contributions	decide a name for the blog	we can buy the domain, and set the webpage	we agree on an appealing name to ensure we attract readers	High	Not Started	Product Owner
006	Industry Contributions	set an initial structure for the blog: domain, storage, webpage	we can start posting articles	we can see an initial webpage up and running	High	Not Started	Product Owner
007	Industry Contributions	post two articles	we can preview how our posts will look like and make changes	we can see two posts published in the webpage with more than 300 words concerning a topic related to leadership or people management	Medium	Not Started	Product Owner
008	Industry Contributions	set connection features like email account, contact form and links to social media	we generate awareness, reach to more people and allow people to connect with us	we have at least 3 different ways for people to connect with us	Medium	Not Started	Product Owner

Sprint I – Sprint Review

The Sprint review will allow us to inspect all the outcomes with the Product Owner and gather feedback in order to create the next set of User Stories for the next Sprint. It is important to have a flexible mentality about this meeting, both from the Product Owner's side and from the Team's side. The Product Owner should expect a high level of quality but not perfection, enough to be able to provide feedback so that User Stories can be continued in the next Sprint with improvements. On the other hand, the team needs to be open to changes. Feedback is always welcome in this methodology since it is what is going to make us deliver products 100% adapted to the current needs of the business. Again, the goal is to deliver User Stories that bring value to the table, if spending too much time on making a User Story perfect is not going to have an impact then we should avoid perfectionism and look for precision and value. Also, when we are estimating User Stories, we estimate the time needed to make the User Story compliant with the definition of "Done", not the time needed to make it perfect. Therefore we must make sure our definition of "Done" is as explicit as possible and to clear out any doubts we have about this definition in order to ensure that what we deliver is bringing the expected value to the table.

Let's see a simple example of perfection vs precision and why we have a strong preference for the latter. Imagine we are discussing task *002 - draft an initial list on courses I could leverage for my professional career*, and the definition of done of this task is *I receive a list of courses with details such as topic, effort, and level of difficulty.*

US 002 – Version 1:

Topic	Course Name	Effort (Time)	Level of difficulty
Analytics	Customer Analytics	5hrs 52min 35sec	3/5

US 002 – Version 2:

Topic	Course Name	Effort (Time)	Level of difficulty
Analytics	Customer Analytics	6 hours approx.	Medium

These two versions are pretty valid outcomes of the task, they are also compliant with the definition of "Done". The first one looks more detailed, perhaps if we were looking for perfection we would have a preference for the first version. But to be honest knowing the number of seconds doesn't add much value, it probably won't change our decision and it might have taken us more time to gather that information. The second version instead, allows us to have a snapshot on the course, and enough information to be able to prioritize correctly, it is compliant with the definition of done and might have taken less time to complete. Finally, each situation will be different, which means that sometimes we will need to add more granularity to our User Stories depending on the goal of the task, therefore my advice is before starting the task we make sure of the following: we are clear on what is the definition of done, we align with the Product Owner on any doubts about what he expects to see, we ask ourselves the level of precision we want to provide, we ask ourselves "what is the real goal of this task?".

Now, let's begin with the Sprint Review, as mentioned before, in order to introduce the User Story, we can rely on these questions:
- The goal of the User Story
- What problems did the team run into (if any)
- What has been the outcome of the User Story
- Inspect the result or piece of work or see an example

US 001 - draft an initial list on ways I can contribute to my industry

The goal of the User Story was to shortlist potential ways to contribute to my industry which can boost my network, improve my brand, and dynamize my relations with companies to which I am a stakeholder or professionals within the industry that were curious and innovative. The list was drafted taking into consideration the impact that this contribution can have in my career in a medium or long-term period and on the other hand the effort to set it up, being the effort and relation between time spent and resources needed. One of the main challenges was to understand not only in which areas I did have expertise but also which areas I actually enjoyed doing, there was no point on showing expertise in something you actually don't like, in addition to that, the list should also allow me to understand which of them required a high effort versus the impact it could have in my career, the synergies it would create, and how it would send the correct message to the market I was targeting. Let's see the list we have drafted and the feedback that will add value to the next delivery of this task. Remember this task can be shared with the Product Owner beforehand, which is something we have chosen to do in order to prepare the set of tasks for the next Sprint.

Contribution	Impact	Effort
Generate content within my areas of expertise	Low	Low
Create an online course about any hard-skill I possess	Medium	Low
Create a website or blog with useful materials, innovative approaches, and tools to solve typical problems in my industry	Medium	High
Publish a book on something I have experience in	High	High
Create a free consultation service for small companies	Medium	High

Feedback: While I was drafting this list I wondered how connected were each one of them with the areas in which I wanted to succeed, but also how easy or difficult were they going to be to maintain over time; meaning how much time were they going to require after the initial structure was set in place. Feedback here is that we need to add two more variables in order to rank these contributions in a sustainable way. We need to add the Sinergy level of the contribution, as how aligned is it with other contributions or my career itself. And on the other hand the Maintenance effort of the contribution, how easy or difficult it will be to maintain over time.

In this experiment I am the Team, the Product Owner, and the Scrum Master at the same time, so I could easily change the table and add those variables. But in a normal Scrum Agile environment, this should be a negotiation between the Team working on this User Story and the Product Owner, since we are changing the requirements of the User Story. This negotiation could be done during the Sprint or as a feedback from the Product Owner in the Sprint Review.

US 003 - draft an initial list of initiatives I would love to launch

The goal of this User Story was not only to draft a list of initiatives that I could run as side projects, but also to satisfy my entrepreneurial spirit, even though I usually work in corporations or start-ups. Sometimes my entrepreneurial background kicks in and makes me wonder if I should develop skills that are related to building something of your own, negotiation, dealing with suppliers, general management, product management. The main challenge of this task was that there were so many different kinds of initiatives I could launch that being able to structure the information correctly took some time. It was also really difficult to know upfront the amount of effort and initial investment that is going to be needed in a way that expectations are managed. Also, it needs to be an initiative that I can launch without having to compromise too much time and that doesn't conflict with my career.

Initiative	Impact	Effort	Investment Needed
Build an online store	Medium	High	Medium
Publish an App	High	Medium	Low
Build a low-cost virtual tutoring service	Medium	High	Low

Feedback: While I was drafting this list, I realized that projects like these take way more than just 1 or 2 hours per day, and it can affect my performance in my other areas that are really important. Also, I need to increase the value it generates for me beyond just satisfying my entrepreneurial spirit, therefore it is important that we assess the synergies it generates with the rest of my career and how I can leverage that experience in different areas. Let's add for the next Sprint the synergies it can create beyond satisfying my curiosity.

US 002 - draft an initial list on courses I could leverage for my professional career

The goal of this User Story was to draft a list of potential courses that could help me add new skills, deep dive in those I needed more experience in, import new knowledge or new approaches to my projects, and last but not least, try new stuff. The time effort would be calculated depending on how many hours per day I should spend to get it done and the difficulty would be rated based on the complexity of the topic.

Topic	Time Effort	Difficulty
Operational Analytics	High	High
Customer Analytics	Medium	Medium
eCommerce	High	Medium
Book Marketing	Low	Low
Facebook and Instagram Marketing	Medium	Medium

Feedback: in this case we don't need further analysis, the goal was to select a few and then start choosing those which we could start immediately to gain momentum.

Sprint I – Sprint Retrospective[10]

Through this book we are going to see different examples of retrospectives. Since this is the first Sprint, let's start with an easy one. Since the Retrospective's goal is to evaluate how we work as a team. With an unbiased as possible analysis of how we can improve the way we execute, I am going to start by analyzing what went well, what I want to improve, and how I am going to act on it.

Went well – To Improve – Action Items Retrospective[11]

Went well	Action items
User Stories were easy to tackle.	Since things have been easy to tackle there is nothing wrong with setting the bar a little bit higher the next Sprint.
Some of the User Stories have allowed us to start making decisions about the Product Backlog.	
	Increase the capacity.
I felt positive that I didn't miss any dependencies that could have blocked us.	Try to proactively gather feedback from User Stories during the Sprint, or even provide ideas if we think they are going to improve the decision-making process.
To improve	
More transparency during the Sprint, probably we could have shared some insights on how things went during the Sprint and not just at the end on the Sprint Review.	Include more Daily Meeting sin the next chapter, this will allow the reader to have more transparency about how the Sprint is going.

---

[10] Source: *Scrum Alliance, https://www.scrumalliance.org/*

[11] Source: *Funretro, https://funretro.io/*

Sprint I – Conclusion

I am positive this Sprint has served to set the basis of the methodology. It has been easy going. The bar wasn't set too high, it got me up and running which is important and I have felt the User Stories were well dimensioned, this usually can be seen on the degree of completion of the Sprint Review vs the Planning. Now that we have set the bases, we need to start setting the bar higher, dedicating more time, focusing on getting tangible work done and pushing projects forward. This will be the goal for the next Sprint.

TIPS FOR EFFECTIVE DAILY MEETINGS

Agile is a pretty flexible methodology, but in order to keep it effective and useful the Daily Meetings need to be very well defined. Even though Daily Meetings have a predefined structure there are some extra tips to make these meetings as effective as possible and keep them that way.

Stand Up!

Even though this first tip might sound funny, the Daily Meeting should always be a standing up meeting. Allowing people to sit down can act as an incentive to spend more time talking, when what we want is simple, straight to the point meetings. When people are standing up in the meeting it creates a feeling of it being a transactional place, it generates a small sense of urgency. Actually, in many places around the world the Daily Meeting is called The Daily Stand Up because of this.

Stick to the script

Sticking to these three questions, what did I do yesterday? What will I spend my time on today? What is blocking me from completing this task on time? It will allow the storyline to be coherent, consistent, and straight to the point. It is encouraged that any topic that needs further discussion is discussed offline. The Scrum Master should coach the team to always stick to these three questions. Believe me, sometimes it will be a challenge, especially when the team has a lot going on.

Sticking to the script is also a matter of empathy. When people stick to the script they make the storyline easy to follow. If team members start talking without structure and go off script the rest of the team starts losing track of what is going on, and therefore reduces the effectiveness of the meeting. Another empathic reason to stick to the script is to respect the time-box for this meeting which should be a maximum of fifteen minutes. If people go off script, the chances are they are going to spend more time than what is necessary to communicate effectively.

Coach the team

One of the main challenges is helping the team adapt to the methodology and the different meetings. The Scrum Master should encourage team members to reach out with any questions they have regarding the methodology. Making people aware that since the methodology is new and flexible nobody should feel ashamed of asking as many questions as they need in order to make the most out of it. Helping or coaching the team before the meetings so that they understand how to make the most out of these is a simple gesture that could help the team and the methodology. One of the most effective ways to do so is by helping team members to polish the storyline for the Daily Meeting. Just by going through the script before the meeting with a person and guide them through what it is encouraged to say and what can be discussed offline.

Make it visual

Using visual tools like a Kanban board in a Daily Meeting, or even during the Sprint Review, can easily help to keep meetings on track and help team members to follow the story line. Putting things in a visual manner also helps the team think how they can tell the story and encourages everybody to follow through on commitment, since when you put something in writing you are in a way making yourself accountable implicitly.

Piggybank

People always seem busy and are always rushing, but in Agile we estimate our tasks in a way that allows us to do our job correctly and without hustling all the time. One of the strong commitments people need to make is arriving on time to meetings. This is not only a matter related to the methodology, it's showing your team members that you do not consider your time more valuable than theirs. Having a team Piggybank to which latecomers should contribute will allow to keep people on time. Worst-case scenario have the latecomers bring beers to the team with the money saved in the Piggybank should be enough.

Lay out the environment your team needs

These meetings are always an opportunity to coach the team in Agile's values in an implicit manner. Encouraging people to speak up when they feel lost, when they feel there is going to be a delay, when they are stuck with an issue, or when they feel blocked in any way is one of the key missions of a Scrum Master. By asking the right questions to the team the Scum Master or Product Owner should be showing their support in helping the team to move forward. This has a lot to do with the concept of Servant Leadership, where Leaders are not only there to take credit but to remove obstacles behind the scenes to ensure teams stay productive and motivated.

Ask the following questions to the team if you feel is necessary, is any stakeholder not answering us? Is there any risk of delay on this or that task? Is anybody struggling with any kind of bureaucracy within the company? Is there any meeting we should schedule to unblock this task? Does X or Y team still need to send us that document or reply to any email to ensure we complete Z User Story? The better we do at asking these questions the more we encourage the team to speak up fearlessly, to stay accountable, and follow through on commitment and to anticipate ourselves as a team to any situation that jeopardizes our performance.

Remind the goal of the Sprint every once in a while

Sprints take usually between two to four weeks. Sometimes the amount of User Stories or the amount of topics that are not linked to each other, or have no relation between each other, can take a toll on the team by making the team forget the real goal of the Sprint and losing sight of what we really want to achieve with the User Story. This brings awareness of the initial goal for that Sprint and helps the team target better where to spend their time and how to tackle User Stories in a way that contribute to achieve the Sprint's initial goal, by doing this you are showing them a bigger picture so that they can judge whether or not another approach is needed for the User Story they are currently working on.

Allow feedback at the end of the meeting

Since the Daily Meeting's goal is to keep everybody aligned, it is encouraged for the Product Owner to provide feedback on the priorities or to provide guidance on how to tackle a User Story from a business perspective. Sometimes the Product Owner will have feedback for more than one team member or more than one User Story. In my experience leaving it until the end allows the meeting to stay on track and moving that feedback to the end doesn't usually affect much on the effectiveness of it. Therefore, as far as possible it is encouraged to leave feedback for the end of the meeting, where the Product Owner can go through different User Stories or Team members providing any valuable feedback that would help prioritizing or tackling any issue regarding User Stories.

Silently evaluate how the team is doing, and start helping them behind the scenes

Scrum Masters need to train and develop an extremely important skill nowadays, listening and listening actively, and we all have room to improve here. By listening to what your team is saying you will be able to understand if the team is overwhelmed, if the team is getting dispersed because of too many different nature User Stories, or understand if they are feeling frustrated about any task in particular and the reason. Scrum Masters should actively listen for signs of frustration in Daily Meetings and then address them when helping the Product Owner when updating the Product Backlog. For instance, something that I have seen in many teams is the team struggling with dispersion, the Product Owner wanting to do many things at the same time that have a different nature. One of the Scrum Master's goals is to help the Product Owner on defining a more consistent Product Backlog that allows the team to focus on less topics or allows team members to specialize in certain areas in order to work more effectively on them.

BREAK CHAPTER

Hey reader! I hope this chapter finds you well, when I started writing this book, little did I know how exciting it would it be to hold the final version in my hands. I remember receiving the first version as if I were a three-year-old receiving a present. I would recommend any of you writing one of your own, chose a topic you love and that you feel you want to build some expertise in and try it, I will be glad to provide with cool tips! I have tried to keep this book as practical and straightforward as possible, which is hard because while I kept on writing I felt like writing even more.

Feel free to contact me if you have any feedback or want to learn more about this powerful framework. I want any reader that feels curious about the methodology to feel free to ask me any question and brainstorm how to implement Agile in their teams, you can now schedule a 30-minute meeting with me scanning this QR code!

And last but not least, I would love it if you could help me spread this methodology by leaving a review on Amazon!

SPRINT II

Sprint II – Planning

The planning meeting for Sprint II can be held the same day as the Sprint Review of Sprint I, it is actually encouraged, this will allow the team to start working on new User Stories immediately. First of all, let's define our goal for this Sprint, we have already discussed a few contribution ideas we can start implementing. Even though we need to complete some User Stories from last Sprint we can set a goal that encourages us to work on materializing some of the contributions we mentioned before.

The goal for this Sprint can be: "Complete assessments and set an initial structure for our industry contributions". Now, let's talk about the capacity, I think we are in a good position to increase the time spent on this next Sprint. One hour per day was very little so for this Sprint we could double the time spent to two hours per day, which would give us 20 hours in total to spend in our projects.

As you may remember during the Refinement Meeting, we were able to go through some of the tasks we were thinking of tackling during this Sprint, let's see what this initially looked like:

ID of Task	Topic or Project	As the Product Owner I want to...	so that...	and I will consider the task as done when...	Priority	Status	Stakeholder(s)
005	Industry Contributions	decide a name for the blog	we can buy the domain, and set the webpage	we agree on an appealing name to ensure we attract readers	High	Not Started	Product Owner
006	Industry Contributions	set an initial structure for the blog: domain, storage, webpage	we can start posting articles	we can see an initial webpage up and running	High	Not Started	Product Owner
007	Industry Contributions	post two articles	we can preview how our posts will look like and make changes	we can see two posts published in the webpage with more than 300 words concerning a topic related to leadership or people management	Medium	Not Started	Product Owner
008	Industry Contributions	set connection features like email account, contact form and links to social media	we generate awareness, reach to more people and allow people to connect with us	we have at least 3 different ways for people to connect with us	Medium	Not Started	Product Owner

In the past Sprint Review we decided that we were keeping two User Stories in the next Sprint in order to complete them with the feedback provided by the Product Owner, User Stories, **US 001 - draft an initial list on ways I can**

81

contribute to my industry and US 003 - draft an initial list of initiatives I would love to launch. After adding these two tasks and another two related to Upskilling, the reason is simple that we might decide to go with writing the book as an industry contribution, therefore these courses can help understand the scope of tasks that are needed to make sure we are doing it correctly. This leaves the following table as a snapshot of the Product Backlog that we will start estimating:

ID of Task	Topic or Project	As the Product Owner I want to...	so that...	and I will consider the task as done when...	Priority	Status	Stakeholder(s)
001	Industry Contributions	draft an initial list on ways I can contribute to my industry	I can shortlist a few to start working on	I receive a list of ways to contribute with details such as effort and impact	High	In Progress	Product Owner
003	Entrepreneurship	draft an initial list on initiatives I would love to launch	I can shortlist a few topics to start working on	I receive a list of topics with details such as impact, effort and investment needed	High	In Progress	Product Owner
005	Industry Contributions	decide a name for the blog	we can buy the domain, and set the webpage	we agree on an appealing name to ensure we attract readers	High	Not Started	Product Owner
006	Industry Contributions	set an initial structure for the blog: domain, storage, webpage	we can start posting articles	we can see an initial webpage up and running	High	Not Started	Product Owner
007	Industry Contributions	post two articles	we can preview how our posts will look like and make changes	we can see two posts published in the webpage with more than 300 words concerning a topic related to leadership or people management	Medium	Not Started	Product Owner
008	Industry Contributions	set connection features like email account, contact form and links to social media	we generate awareness, reach to more people and allow people to connect with us	we have at least 3 different ways for people to connect with us	Medium	Not Started	Product Owner
009	Upskilling	do a course related to kindle self-publishing	we can leverage that knowledge when drafting our eBook	course is completed	Medium	Not Started	Product Owner
010	Upskilling	do a course related to eBook marketing	we can leverage the knowledge to promote and divulge the book	course is completed and a list of marketing actions is drafted as next steps for the book's promotion	Medium	Not Started	Product Owner

Now that we have decided the Sprint's goal, the capacity, and the list of User Stories that are eligible to be included in the planning, let's start estimating. This time we are going to deep dive into a few examples on how we can estimate the time it is going to take us and how to decide the final estimation. Remember in a normal Sprint planning this should be reasoned negotiation between the Team that is working on the task.

Remember the variables you might need to have in consideration in order to ensure a thorough estimation:

- Any analysis that needs to be done beforehand and that can delay the task

- Any dependencies on other teams that need to be untangled
- The complexity of the task and the risk of not having reliable sources of information on time
- Understanding clearly what the Product Owner wants to see and in which format
- Understanding the impact of these tasks in any other teams or current processes (or systems)

US 001 - draft an initial list on ways I can contribute to my industry

As you may recall, this task has been dragged from the previous Sprint. The feedback has been that we need to add synergy levels of each contribution to my career and, how easy or difficult it was to maintain over time. Let's go back again to the current snapshot of the User Story.

Contribution	Impact	Effort
Generate content within my areas of expertise	Low	Low
Create an online course about any hard-skill I possess	Medium	Low
Create a website or blog with useful materials, innovative approaches and tools to solve typical problems in my industry	Medium	High
Publish a book on something I have experience in	High	High
Create a free consultation service for small companies	Medium	High

Based on this table and current knowledge of each topic we could say that assessing how aligned a contribution is with my career is a quick judgment and doesn't need much research right now, perhaps 30 minutes would be enough to make this assessment. On the other hand I would say that I do need to do some research about the maintenance implications for the book, also the maintenance implications on generating content within areas of expertise and the blog. This research would take me around one or two hours; based on all the above, I am torn between estimating two or two and a half hours in total for this User Story. Since the synergy assessment might not even take more than 30 minutes, I am going to go with two hours in total for this User Story.

Could we go with two and a half? Yes, and the Product Owner should understand it, one of the main values of Agile is trusting the team on their judgement about the time spent on the tasks. Our Teams are experts in understanding the steps needed to complete the task and therefore we should trust them whilst making the whole team accountable for productivity. Further in the book we will see ways in which the Scrum Master can help the Product Owner, ensuring productivity and performance of the methodology.

US 005 - decide a name for the blog

This task will require a little bit of research, I would like to find a name that is appealing to my target readers, professionals between twenty-five and forty-five years, usually living in big cities, and that operate in environments which are constantly changing. Also, I need to do some research on keywords to decide the best name. Still, I don't want to go crazy at this stage about this, even though it will be necessary in order to choose the domain name, or the Instagram account, it can later be changed at little or no cost. Assigning one hour to do some keyword research should be fine.

US 006 - set an initial structure for the blog: domain, storage, webpage

In general the task should involve buying a domain, setting up the module that will host the blog, preparing an initial structure for the blog, installing a nice and minimalistic theme, this could take around four hours. In addition to this we should make ourselves the questions mentioned above.

- Any analysis that needs to be done beforehand and that can delay the task? I think we do need to prepare an initial structure to start with, a structure for the blog, simple and minimalistic but modern and straight to each of the topics I want to cover. This design thinking can take around one hour.
- Any dependencies on other teams that need to be untangled? Right now, there are no dependencies.
- Any hidden complexity of the task or the risk of not having reliable sources of information on time? We are not currently relying on external information to deliver this User Story.
- Understanding clearly what the Product Owner wants to see and in which format. This one certainly will take some time to complete,

seeing a prototype and then making a few changes could take two or three hours.

- Understanding the impact of these tasks in any other teams or current processes (or systems), right now there is no impact whatsoever.

The four hours that we have estimated and the considerations above sum around 6 hours, which should be enough to achieve a tangible outcome for this User Story.

Now that we have seen a few examples of how User Stories are estimated let's see how the Sprint Plans looks like for Sprint II.

Sprint Goal: Complete assessments and set an initial structure for our industry contributions			
Sprint End-Date: 29/11			
		Capacity (in hours)	20
Task ID	Task Name (User Story)	Team Estimation	Capacity Left
001	draft an initial list on ways I can contribute to my industry (alignment and maintenance)	2	18
003	draft an initial list on initiatives I would love to launch (add synergy)	2	16
005	decide on a name for the blog	1	15
006	set an initial structure for the blog: domain, storage, webpage	6	9
007	post two articles	4	5
008	set connection features like email account, contact form, and links to social media	2.5	2.5
009	take a course related to kindle self-publishing	3	-0.5

Sprint II – Daily Meetings

Day 2.

- What did I do yesterday? *Yesterday, I added the level of alignment and maintenance to the contributions list, completing the task*
- What will I spend my time on today? *I will work on adding synergy level to the initiatives I want to launch*

- What is blocking me from completing this task on time? *Nothing, right now*

Day 4.
- What did I do yesterday? *Yesterday, I was able to research and decide the name for the blog, millennial office, and start setting the initial structure, buying the domain, setting up the webpage and the initial structure*
- What will I spend my time on today? *Today, I will work on the structure and setting the menus and sections of the blog*
- What is blocking me from completing this task on time? *Right now, the only roadblock I see is that the themes to use for the structure are not exactly what I need, so trying to decide the best theme for the blog is taking more time, also the structure of the blog is suitable for the short term, meaning it's only prepared to post articles. I might need to change a few things in order to make it easier to maintain over time, perhaps adding a section where readers can refer to the books I have published or the courses I am preparing.*

In this case, since I am acting as Product Owner and team, I will have to make a decision on which theme to use and which structure better suits our public and our publications. But, in Agile teams, the Team will be working in the solution and will need guidance from the Product Owner, which knows better the needs from the business side.

Day 6.
- What did I do yesterday? *Yesterday, I was able to complete the initial structure, including menus and sections.*
- What will I spend my time on today? *Today, I want to focus on setting the home page's structure and updating all the information needed to prepare the website for the launch, logos, contact information, titles, and subtitles. Also, I want to start doing the research about the two articles we are going to publish as a test.*
- What is blocking me from completing this task on time? *I would like to see different examples on how others have structured their blog, or*

homepage. This would allow me to get different perspectives and decide the home page I like most and that is state of the art.

In these kinds of situations, the team will need to work collaboratively with the Product Owner to find structures on pages that incorporate the latest ideas or features in order to decide whether they need to include them. Working together will also provide the Product Owner ideas about the User Stories for the next Sprint.

Day 8.

- What did I do yesterday? *Yesterday, I posted two articles related to topics that the blog would cover, in this case one was about dealing with procrastination and the other about servant leadership. They are already posted at the website.*
- What will I spend my time on today? *I will start setting the connections from the website to social media and setting the different accounts that make sense for the type of professional blog we are building.*
- What is blocking me from completing this task on time? *We need to confirm which social networks we are going to use to spread our message.*

At the end of this Daily Meeting there are two User Stories that need some input from the Product Owner. On one hand, the User Story *007 – post two articles*, has been completed and should be reviewed by the Product Owner, since in Agile we operate with minimum viable products there is a chance there will be feedback and that there will be new user stories to polish how we see the articles in our website. In the next chapter we will talk about MVP concept and how it changes the way we work versus traditional approaches. On the other hand, for User Story 008 - *set connection features like email account, contact form, and links to social media*, the Team will need to make decisions on the go. These decisions can be changed in the future, since setting social networks is free and we don't need to make a whole project out of it, therefore the smart thing to do would be to align with the Product Owner on which social networks we want to create and link initially, in Agile Methodologies revisiting this User Story in the future and adding more social networks would be totally admissible.

Sprint II – Refinement Meeting

The Refinement Meeting this Sprint is happening a few days before the Sprint Review, specifically in day 8, in this Sprint we will follow this agenda:

- We will go through the tasks that should be delivered by the end of the Sprint and realign expectations, also we will talk about any roadblocks that have stopped us from finishing or starting any of the tasks in our planning. – 20 minutes
- The Product Owner will go through the tasks planned for the next Sprint so that the team can make the necessary due diligence to provide precise estimations on the planning meeting. – 20 minutes

Let's start with the tasks that ought to be delivered by the end of the Sprint and their status. As you may remember the possible outcomes can be, "done", "blocked", "delayed", "not started", "not finished" or perhaps any of these with a comment and we want to keep the not started or not finished to a minimum.

Task ID	Task Name (User Story)	Status
001	draft an initial list on ways I can contribute to my industry (alignment and maintenance)	Done
003	draft an initial list on initiatives I would love to launch (add synergy)	Done
005	decide a name for the blog	Done
006	set an initial structure for the blog: domain, storage, webpage	Done
007	post two articles	Done
008	set connection features like email account, contact form, and links to social media	Done
009	take a course related to kindle self-publishing	Not Finished

Since the Product Owner has been connected with the team in the Daily Meetings and sharing the outcomes of each task, the Product Backlog can be updated to start tackling the changes that we want to implement to our current MVPs, let's see some of the User Stories that we want to start working on the next Sprint:

ID of Task	Topic or Project	As the Product Owner I want to...	so that...	and I will consider the task as done when...	Priority	Status	Stakeholder(s)
011	Industry Contributions	add a newsletter form in at least two pages	visitors can register for updates	the form is visible and tested	Medium	Not Started	Product Owner
012	Industry Contributions	populate the blog with some relevant pictures	the blog starts having a visual effect in visitors	we see relevant pictures in the home page of the blog	Medium	Not Started	Product Owner
013	Industry Contributions	test all social media connections	we confirm all channels are reachable and visually appealing	we have linked Instagram, Facebook and Medium correctly and with some content posted	High	Not Started	Product Owner
014	Industry Contributions	make visual changes to the pages where articles are posted	anything we post is easy to read, interact and share	article pages are visible, shareable on social media, and disposition looks like other state of the art blogs	High	Not Started	Product Owner

Sprint II – Sprint Review

Now that we have started working on tangible projects let's start reviewing different User Stories and try to simulate how a Sprint Review with feedback on the spot would look like.

US 001 - draft an initial list on ways I can contribute to my industry

As mentioned above, this task has been dragged from the previous Sprint, the feedback was that we needed to add synergy levels of each contribution to my career and, how easy or difficult it was to maintain over time.

Contribution	Impact	Effort	Synergy	Maintenance
Generate content within my areas of expertise	Low	Low	High	Medium
Create an online course about any hard-skill I possess	Medium	Medium	Medium	Low
Create a website or blog with useful materials, innovative approaches and tools to solve typical problems in my industry	Medium	High	High	Medium
Publish a book on something I have experience in	High	High	High	Medium
Create a free consultation service for small companies	Medium	High	Medium	High

Feedback: we want to shortlist those options that make sense to my career, therefore we need to understand which options have the highest impact and synergy with the lowest maintenance. About the effort, I really think something that provides value will require some effort, and it will probably be worth it. If we shortlist the options with high-medium impact first, low-medium maintenance second, and synergy level third we have the following:

Contribution	Impact	Effort	Synergy	Maintenance
Create an online course about any hard-skill I possess	Medium	Medium	Medium	Low
Create a website or blog with useful materials, innovative approaches, and tools to solve typical problems in my industry	Medium	High	High	Medium
Publish a book on something I have experience in	High	High	High	Medium

In order to keep my contributions as consistent as possible with my professional goals, from now on, we are going to focus in the short-medium term on this final list:

Contribution	Impact	Effort	Synergy	Maintenance
Create a website or blog with useful materials, innovative approaches, and tools to solve typical problems in my industry	Medium	High	High	Medium
Publish a book on something I have experience in	High	High	High	Medium

The rest of the contributions can be done later. Remember, there is a high-level roadmap that can be modified, but for us what is important right now is to know where to focus our strengths on. In regard to this User Story, we have achieved our goal which was to shortlist suitable industry contributions and therefore we can mark it as Done in our Product Backlog[12].

US 003 - draft an initial list of initiatives I would love to launch

This User Story was also carried from the previous Sprint, the changes we were going to make were adding the level of synergy between the initiatives with our career priorities, the list now looks this way:

Initiative	Impact	Effort	Investment Needed	Synergy
Build an online store	Medium	High	Medium	Low
Publish an App	High	Medium	Medium	Medium
Build a low-cost virtual tutoring service	Medium	High	Low	Medium

---

[12] Source: *Scrum Alliance, https://www.scrumalliance.org/*

We can easily shortlist the initiatives based on the impact, synergy, effort, and investment needed, respectively, or if you wish based on another order. In this case I am going to go with the one that has the highest impact and the highest synergy level with my career, which is Publish an App, why is it that has the highest impact and synergy level? I have always worked in Technology and Operations, therefore always have been relatively close to product, even helping Product Managers, therefore publishing an App could give me valuable experience in dealing with software development teams, testing, handling requirements or features, and reporting bugs. Also, Agile Methodologies are usually very linked to technology teams, therefore having experience in handling priorities of a technological product can be extremely handy.

US 006 - set an initial structure for the blog: domain, storage, webpage

The goal of this task was to build the initial structure for the blog, we needed to research domains, buy the correct plan and set up the initial structure that would allow us to start building the structure, for this initial structure we created different sections that we will start populating over time:

- Home section, with the updates, social media links, perhaps some visual content
- Articles, which would be used as the main blogging section
- White Papers, where I would post specific reports or case studies that would help companies solve specific problems or challenges
- Resources, where I would post tangible resources like courses or books
- About Me, that would show information about me as a professional, author, and entrepreneur
- Contact, that would allow people to connect with me

What relevant issues did we ran into? I think the only one worth mentioning was the lack of free templates for what I wanted to do, so in order to start preparing the structure I went ahead with one that had a great home page, but we might find out that the other pages need intensive work to make them useful to our needs.

Feedback: now that we have an initial structure, we want to start preparing a few sections for which we have information already, the contact section, about me section, and articles sections should start having content.

US 007 – post two articles

The goal of this task was to publish two initial articles to start seeing what they looked like and what changes we wanted to make. Let's see a few snapshots of this User Story.

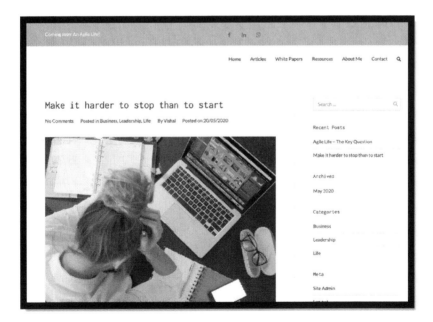

Agile Life – The Key Question

Make it harder to stop than to start

Archives

May 2020

Categories

Business

Leadership

Life

Meta

Site Admin

Log out

Entries feed

Comments feed

WordPress.org

I was having a slice of pizza at a well-known restaurant at Neal's Yard, I was sitting there with one of the owners of a startup in London I had invested in and wanted to know more about what pain points the owners were running into when executing projects with a very limited budget, my goal was to understand how could Agile Methodologies help them in executing better and with a constrained budget and a unstructured team, whilst achieving their goals. They have already raised some funds from small investors and they weren't in a position to increase substantially their budget via fundraising in order to bring in senior professionals to execute projects, but without seniority they felt these initiatives were becoming too big to handle, but even before handling, they were becoming too big to structure which meant team members had a hard time understanding where to start and how to follow when something got blocked, they weren't being able to dedicate time to support their teams and therefore the lack of guidance was affecting the timelines.

effort and do have some impact, you might find out that you were procrastinating because of the structure and magnitude of the problems and not because you were being lazy. The Scrum Master can use this as a guide to take action whenever it feels right based on these guidelines, one of the main responsibilities of a Scrum Master is to remove any impediments that the team has but, by using this approach not only we are removing impediments but also dynamizing our relation between the Team, Product Owner and stakeholders.

Agile Life - The Key Question >

Leave a Reply

Logged in as Vishal. Log out?

Comment

Post Comment

Feedback: The title needs to be centered and with a different font, the metadata that is being showed should be hidden. The text body should be justified. We need to add links to share to social media, the left bar needs to be hidden, and we need to provide ways in which people can subscribe, interact, and contact me. Also, we need to make the post more appealing with charts, tables, or more images.

Sprint II – Sprint Retrospective

For this Sprint I have chosen the Academy Awards Retrospective[13], which is a fun retrospective to classify which User Stories we have enjoyed, which ones have added more value, and which ones have been a pain for us. To make it funnier you could bring some prizes for the person who worked in the winner User Stories.

Best User Story
post two articles

I decided that US 007 – post two articles was the best User Story because it was the one that allowed me to start doing some research and understand what it took to maintain the blog. Also, by posting them I was able to see how things started to look, and will probably generate many new User Stories to improve the visibility in order to make every post appealing to my readers.

Most Exciting User Story
set an initial structure for the blog: domain, storage, webpage

Setting the initial structure was without a doubt the most exciting User Story, because it allowed me to feel like things were starting to materialize. Being able to see a tangible outcome and seeing it live really helped feel like we were moving forward.

Most Annoying User Story
take a course related to kindle self-publishing

The most annoying User Story is without of doubt the passive one, the User Story was necessary to understand better the implications of writing a book,

[13] Source: *Funretro, https://funretro.io/*

and it had important points to have in consideration. But in general this User Story felt slow and I ended up doing it at the gym while I was cycling.

Sprint II – Conclusion

In this Sprint we have made huge progress in what relates to productivity and generating the environment to move forward. We have been able to make the necessary decisions so that we could start building a consistent product backlog and started delivering tangible outcomes of our work. Now it is time to speed up, deliver more and add a ton of value each Sprint. We have also seen the outcomes of a few User Stories and these results allows us to have feedback that can be turned into new User Stories. We will see in the Planning Meeting that besides the User Stories proposed at the Refinement Meeting in this Sprint, we have decided to add a few more based on the Sprint review we just had.

CASE IV. AGILE ENABLING SERVANT LEADERSHIP

Servant leadership goes hand in hand in Agile. Scrum Masters are in a unique position to manage the progress of the project but also to help the individual team members of the team to ensure that the requirements are met, to perform well, and reduce the risk of burnouts. The main goal of servant leadership is for the leader to serve the team by prioritizing his team, the client, and the project first. Servant leaders serve by removing blockers that can hamper the performance of his team and help his teammates overcome challenges and impediments. They also prioritize customer satisfaction by ensuring that clients are kept up to date on the progress of the project as well as asking for feedback and suggestions from the client.

It's important for servant leaders to operate behind the scenes with integrity, putting the team's interest above their own interests. But also for companies to recognize the value that these leaders bring to the table. They are not looking to take credit, they are not looking to show off and look busy, they are operating behind the scenes to make sure people are productive and happy.

The Qualities and Characteristics of a Servant Leader

A servant leader must have a serve-first mindset and other important qualities that focuses on helping improve and empower his team or their employees.

Listening

Servant leaders must be able to listen to their team members, the people around them, or their employees. Listening is an important skill for a leader in general so it is one of the top qualities a servant leader should possess.

Empathy

Being empathic to team members, subordinates, and employees allows great leaders to better understand the different perspectives of their team members and employees.

Healing

A good servant leader must be able to create and maintain great relationships with their team members or employees. Servant leaders must also be able to mend and heal the morale and emotional health of their subordinates or employees.

Awareness

Self-awareness is also one of the important qualities a servant leader should possess. Knowing the strengths will allow great leaders to improve their existing skillsets. Identifying weaknesses and limitations will allow leaders to find ways to improve on them and increase their chances of success as a leader.

Persuasion

Possessing the skill of persuasion will allow leaders to inspire their subordinates, team members, and employees into action. Great leaders do not use their authority and power to force people to follow but instead use charisma and the power of persuasion.

Conceptualization

The ability to conceptualize thoughts into ideas that the team members and employees can easily understand is a helpful quality that will allow leaders to easily share their long-term visions and short-term goals.

Foresight

Being able to anticipate events by observing what is happening and using past experiences will allow leaders to gain foresight on a rapidly changing project, business trends, or the weather in the markets. Foresight allows leaders to quickly adapt to changes by anticipating events based on their experience and observations.

Stewardship

Stewardship is the quality of going beyond just managing team members and employees. Being a steward means that leaders should be willing to help their team members and employees grow personally and professionally. Stewardship puts the interest of employees above the grueling balance of profit margins.

Commitment to the Growth of People

Commitment to the growth of people is one of the cornerstone qualities of a servant leader. A leader must be able to foster positive growth personally and professionally through coaching, training, and activities that help promote learning.

How Servant Leadership can be Applied to Business in General

Practicing servant leadership in the real world may seem to be a daunting task but with the right mindset, drive, and dedication it can easily be accomplished. In an Agile environment, the project manager or Scrum Master not only leads the team but also serves the team and its team members by ensuring that the team is performing efficiently by actively interacting and coaching team members.

Serving the team by coaching and mentoring team members helps them grow and reach their full potential. A good leader adds value to individual team members and the team as a whole by helping them develop new skills and enhance existing skills. Mentoring also helps team members overcome challenges and solve problems that are faced by the project.

Provide the team the confidence to overcome obstacles and inspire them to complete the tasks to the best of their abilities. Serving as a driving inspiration for the team requires a degree of self-confidence and charisma. They also help build and maintain relationships with and between team members to ensure that the team functions as a unit. They also deal with conflict that may arise between team members and are the arbitrators to peacefully and quickly resolve conflict.

Complete tasks and meet deadlines on time by prioritizing tasks. Servant leaders must be result-oriented and are able to balance the workload of team members to maximize productivity and reduce the risk of burnout. They are responsible for ensuring that their team members have the right resources and information available to complete their job properly and efficiently. Servant Leaders are able to delegate tasks properly and share the workload with the rest of the team members to help cultivate responsibility and teamwork. They value the contributions of the team and also ensure that credit is given to where credit is due to help foster a sense of achievement amongst the team members and inspire the team as a whole.

They also serve as a bridge between the team, the upper management, and the client. They ensure that all parties involved have the appropriate actionable information about the project at all times and are able to get feedback and direction from the respective parties. The servant leaders serve by ensuring that the team members can focus on their respective tasks by handling client interactions and company politics.

With great leadership comes great service

Cultivating Servant Leadership allows leaders to actively take part in their team. They contribute by serving the team and its team members through coaching, mentoring, and building professional relationships. They empower their team members by inspiring them to grow professionally by ensuring that they have the right resources and training to perform well. All in all, they ensure that the welfare of their team is prioritized above all aspects of the project to allow them to tackle obstacles and challenges faced by the project.

How servant leadership can be applied to business in general

Practicing servant leadership in the real world may seem to be a daunting task but with the right mindset, drive, and dedication it can easily be accomplished. In an Agile environment, the project manager or Scrum Master not only leads the team but also serves the team and its team members by ensuring that the team is performing efficiently by actively interacting and coaching team members. Serving the team by coaching and mentoring team members helps them grow and reach their full potential. A good leader adds value to individual team members and the team as a whole by helping them develop new skills and enhance existing skills. Mentoring also helps team members overcome challenges and solve problems that are faced by the project.

They also help build and maintain relationships with and between team members to ensure that the team functions as a unit. They also deal with conflict that may arise between team members and are the arbitrators to peacefully and quickly resolve conflict.

Servant Leaders are able to delegate tasks properly and share the workload with the rest of the team members to help cultivate responsibility and teamwork. They value the contributions of the team and also ensure that credit is given to where credit is due to help foster a sense of achievement amongst the team members and inspire the team as a whole. They complete tasks and meet deadlines on time by prioritizing tasks. Servant leaders must be result-oriented and are able to balance the workload of team members to maximize productivity and reduce the risk of burnout. They are responsible for ensuring that their team members have the right resources and information available to complete their job properly and efficiently.

SPRINT III

Sprint III – Planning

Now that we have decided which projects we are going to stick with, we need to start driving them forward. In this book we are going to cover six Sprints, and we should be able to look back and see substantial achievements, again, keeping in mind we are dedicating a small amount of time per day. In order to define the goal for this Sprint let's outline the main initiatives we have shortlisted as our priorities:

Industry Contributions:

Contribution	Impact	Effort	Synergy	Maintenance
Create a website or blog with useful materials, innovative approaches, and tools to solve typical problems in my industry	Medium	High	High	Medium
Publish a book on something I have experience in	High	High	High	Medium

Initiatives:

Initiative	Impact	Effort	Investment Needed	Synergy
Publish an App	High	Medium	Medium	Medium

Now, what goal should we set? We are already working on the website; we want to structure the book and at least have a mockup of the app that we want to develop by the end of this Sprint, we also want to start researching developers that can help us with our limited budget app. Based on all the above we can conclude the goal is "Prepare the blog for launch in all sections in which I have relevant content to post, draft initial requirements for the app, and initial structure for the book". Once the goal is set we need to align the capacity, we started the first Sprint with 1 hour per day, the second Sprint we ramped up to 2 hours per day. I feel that this Sprint we will need more dedication, 3 hours per day should be enough. Remember you can adjust the capacity as you wish, three hours is just the amount of time I see reasonable given the amount of work we have but taking into consideration that we have other responsibilities.

As you may remember during the past Refinement Meeting, we went through some of the tasks we were thinking on tackling during this Sprint, let's see what this initially looked like:

ID of Task	Topic or Project	As the Product Owner I want to...	so that...	and I will consider the task as done when...	Priority	Status	Stakeholder(s)
011	Industry Contributions	add a newsletter form in at least two pages	visitors can register for updates	the form is visible and tested	Medium	Not Started	Product Owner
012	Industry Contributions	populate the blog with some relevant pictures	the blog starts having a visual effect in visitors	we see relevant pictures in the home page of the blog	Medium	Not Started	Product Owner
013	Industry Contributions	test all social media connections	we confirm all channels are reachable and visually appealing	we have linked Instagram, Facebook and Medium correctly and with some content posted	High	Not Started	Product Owner
014	Industry Contributions	make visual changes to the pages where articles are posted	anything we post is easy to read, interact and share	article pages are visible, shareable on social media, and disposition looks like other state of the art blogs	High	Not Started	Product Owner

In order to achieve our goal, we need to add new User Stories and rearrange the priorities that we have defined, some of the User Stories we have set as high priority will fall into a medium priority or even a low. For instance, *US 011 – add a newsletter form in at least two pages,* has become less of a priority since there is still no content, whereas test all social media connections is still important but not a priority right now. Since we have a basic structure the priority should be setting up the content that can be used already.

ID of Task	Topic or Project	As the Product Owner I want to...	so that...	and I will consider the task as done when...	Priority	Status	Stakeholder(s)
015	Industry Contributions	publish initial "About Me" section	visitors can understand the background and the context for my contributions	we have an initial "About Me" section which is appealing	High	Not Started	Product Owner
016	Industry Contributions	complete the design of the home page	the initial eye impact of the blog captures people's attention	we have an initial Home Page that is modern, visible and adaptable to changes	High	Not Started	Product Owner
017	Industry Contributions	prepare the initial structure for the book	we can start working immediately on the content	we draft an initial structure that meet's the following: current topics are covered, increases my professional value, generates branding, I enjoy writing, practical and applicable	High	Not Started	Product Owner
018	Initiatives	prepare a mockup of an app I would like to publish	we can start drafting the features we want to include	we can see a mockup of the app we want to publish	High	Not Started	Product Owner
019	Initiatives	prepare a list of features for this initial version of the app	we can start developing these requirements with the software developers	we have defined at least the basic features of the app, sign-up, login and feed	Medium	Not Started	Product Owner
011	Industry Contributions	add a newsletter form in at least two pages	visitors can register for updates	the form is visible and tested	Low	Not Started	Product Owner
012	Industry Contributions	populate the blog with some relevant pictures	the blog starts having a visual effect in visitors	we see relevant pictures in the home page of the blog	Low	Not Started	Product Owner
013	Industry Contributions	test all social media connections	we confirm all channels are reachable and visually appealing	we have linked Instagram, Facebook and Medium correctly and with some content posted	Medium	Not Started	Product Owner
014	Industry Contributions	make visual changes to the pages where articles are posted	anything we post is easy to read, interact and share	article pages are visible, shareable on social media, and disposition looks like other state of the art blogs	High	Not Started	Product Owner

Now that we have updated the Product Backlog it is time to start estimating User Stories, let's see a few examples:

US 009 – take a course related to kindle self-publishing

This task has been carried from the previous Sprint, it had already been started and we just need to complete it. Since most of the course was completed, around 70%, the estimation for this task has been set to around one hour.

US 015 – publish initial "About Me" section

Let's start by responding to the questions we need to make ourselves before estimating this task.

- Is there any analysis that needs to be done beforehand and that can delay the task? We do need to do some analysis and research on other blogs that we find appealing and that have the latest features and that are as visual as possible. This will take a few hours, it shouldn't take more than two.

- Are there any dependencies on other teams that need to be untangled? We do need to take some pictures for this, so we might need to hire someone or ask a friend and look for a nice location to do them.
- Is there any complexity hidden in this task or any risk of not having reliable sources of information on time? Not that we know of, we have all the information we need.
- What does the Product Owner want to see and in which format? What we want to see is an appealing about me section, that is state of the art, that shows all experiences, knowledge that I have achieved during my years of professional experience but also showing the brands I have worked for and the major achievements. We want to show this in different ways; teams I have managed, stakeholders I have liaised with, and all this in a visual manner that is easy to follow and read through.
- Is there an impact of these tasks in any other teams or current processes (or systems)? Not right now.

With all this in consideration I feel one or two hours to do some research on good looking "About Me" sections to get good ideas; two hours to complete my basic information, education and experience; one hour to set up the brands section; two hours to include complementary information like team management, soft-skills, a skill-matrix; and finally one or two hours to format changes, rearrangement of widgets and minor content changes. Also, from the analysis above we have realized that we need pictures, therefore this should translate into a new User Story. It wouldn't block us, but ideally, we want to do it as soon as possible.

US 014 – make visual changes to the pages where the articles are posted

The feedback of the User Story 007 was that the title needed to be centered and with a different font, the metadata that was being shown should be hidden, also the text body should be justified. We needed to add links to share to social media, the left bar needed to be hidden, and we had to provide ways in which people can subscribe, interact, and contact me. Also, we had to make the post more appealing with charts, tables, or more images. In addition to this, we should design the page so that articles stacked up in a visible manner and they are easy to preview, this probably will mean doing some research for a widget that allows us to do it. See estimations below.

Change	Estimation (hrs.)
Title design	0,25
Font selection	0,25
Hide metadata and select relevant metadata	0,5
Add links to social media, design, and test	1
Design of left bar	0,5
Subscription options, newsletter	1
Contact options	0,5
Charts, tables, and images	0,5
Design of article page	1,5

US 017 – prepare the initial structure of the book

Our goal is to contribute to the industry in a topic where there is still a lot of lack of knowledge and where we are well positioned to contribute. In this case I see a lot of potential on writing a book about how using Agile Methodologies I was able to drive my projects forward by only dedicating a few hours per day and leveraging the tools that Agile Methodologies provided to ensure progress and flexible execution. I would like to make it a practical playbook and with practical cases where the methodology can help leaders to solve ambiguous problems where there is no right or wrong answer but ways to proceed. Let start making ourselves the questions to estimate the bandwidth of this User Story.

- Is there any analysis that needs to be done beforehand and that can delay the task? We do need to see a few examples on how normal books are structured, besides our chapters, each book usually has a few introductory chapters that lead to the main story.
- Are there any dependencies on other teams that need to be untangled? Right now, we can move on with an initial structure without any risk of dependencies since we are only going to focus on an initial structure and not content.
- Is there any complexity hidden in this task or any risk of not having reliable sources of information on time? Yes, the chapters need to follow a story line and we need to define what we want to tell, how to tell it, and who is going to be our target reader. Also, the book needs

to have a playbook structure and be practical, therefore it should look like a project.

- What does the Product Owner want to see and in which format? The expected outcome of this task is to have a list of the initial structure of the book and high-level content for each chapter. We will also show any introductory chapter or any section, despite it being part of the main body or not. For instance, if we want to save the initial part of the book to make any acknowledgment, we should show it in the structure.
- Is there an impact of these tasks in any other teams or current processes (or systems)? Not right now.

Task within User Story	Estimation (hrs.)
Examples and research on book structures	1
Draft initial list of chapters	1,5
Define high-level content for each chapter	1,5

After having estimated all tasks, let's see what the planning for this Sprint looks like:

Sprint Goal: Prepare the blog for launch in all sections in which I have relevant content to post, draft initial requirements for the app and initial structure for the book			
Sprint End-Date: 13/12			
		Capacity (in hours)	30
Task ID	Task Name (User Story)	Team Estimation (hours)	Capacity Left
009	take a course related to kindle self-publishing	1	29
015	publish initial "About Me" section	8	21
016	complete the design of the home page	9	12
014	make visual changes to the pages where articles are posted	6	6
017	prepare the initial structure for the book	4	2
018	prepare a mockup of an app I would like to publish	4	-2

Sprint III – Daily Meetings

As usual, the Daily Meetings start from the second day of the Sprint onwards if we hold them in the morning. But if you decided to hold the Daily Meeting at the end of the day then it would be possible to have one the first day, since the goal is to share updates there is no point on having it the first day if there aren't any. Remember these meetings should take between ten to fifteen minutes and there is a predefined script.

Day 2.

- What did I do yesterday? *I completed the course about kindle self-publishing and started researching "About Me" sections of known influencers.*
- What will I spend my time on today? *I will start preparing a mockup design for the "About Me" section, which is one of the most important ones, and consolidating all the information I want to post there.*
- What is blocking me from completing this task on time? *Right now, nothing.*

Day 3.

- What did I do yesterday? *I prepared a mockup structure for the "About Me" section and started building a prototype with different aspects of my career.*
- What will I spend my time on today? *I will keep working on the prototype for the "About Me" section, including in the page credentials, references, contributions, experience, and skills.*
- What is blocking me from completing this task on time? *The text editor of the webpage is giving me a hard time, and I am seeing myself with three different kind of fonts in the same page, which makes it look inconsistent and uneven. I will have to spend some time going section by section ensuring everything has the same format.*

Day 4.

- What did I do yesterday? *Completed most of the topics inside the "About Me" section, we are still missing the education and skills area, which I will start working on today.*
- What will I spend my time on today? *Work on the education and skills area inside the "About Me" section.*

- What is blocking me from completing this task on time? *I still haven't got a clear picture of how I am going to show my skillset in a way that is easy to read and understand by any reader. These skills are somehow technical and can be confusing to many of the visitors, so it won't be only about showing the skillset but also making sure they are easy to understand.*

This User Story is already behind schedule, and therefore as a team we need to assess if we need to reduce the scope of this task in this Sprint or complete it regardless of the impact it will have on the subsequent tasks following this one. We will probably go with a mix of both, I would let the Product Owner know about the situation and then realign the expectations of this task and agree on having a task on the next Sprint that follows up to this one. The feedback in this case would be to consolidate the information about skills and education but not to post it in the "About Me" section yet.

Day 6.
- What did I do yesterday? *I researched different blog pages to gather ideas on how to show the home page looking even, dynamic, and as up to date as possible.*
- What will I spend my time on today? *My goal today is to settle an initial structure of the home page that will generate awareness of the different sections, and that provides the journey I expect the visitor to follow.*
- What is blocking me from completing this task on time? *We need to decide which journey we expect visitors to have, which sections are the most important, and what will be appealing to external viewers, that might differ from what it appealing to me.*

At this point, as Product Owner, and anticipating we won't be able to finish all the tasks in the Sprint, I am going to rearrange the priorities, ranking lower US 014, and prioritizing US 017- prepare the initial structure of the book. The reason? Improving the pages where we are posting articles is not as urgent as we thought, we are not launching it and when we launch it we will probably do it alongside the book. Therefore it is more important to improve the main sections of the webpage, like the Home Page or the "About Me" section than improving the blog section. In addition to this, starting to define the eBook structure could help us unblock tasks for the next Sprint. Having said this, let's see a snapshot on what the Sprint Plan looks like with this last-minute change:

Task ID	Task Name (User Story)	Team Estimation (hours)	Capacity Left
009	take a course related to kindle self-publishing	1	29
015	publish initial "About Me" section	8	21
016	complete the design of the home page	9	12
017	prepare the initial structure for the book	4	8
018	prepare a mockup of an app I would like to publish	4	4
014	make visual changes to the pages where articles are posted	6	-2

Sprint III – Refinement Meeting

The Refinement Meeting this Sprint is happening a few days before the Sprint Review, specifically in day 8. In this Sprint we will follow this agenda:

- We will go through the tasks that should be delivered by the end of the Sprint and realign expectations, also we will talk about any roadblocks that have stopped us from finishing or starting any of the tasks in our planning. – 20 minutes
- Review the current backlog, update priorities, and go through the tasks planned for the next Sprint so that the team can make the necessary due diligence to provide precise estimations on the planning meeting. – 30 minutes

Let's start with the tasks that ought to be delivered by the end of the Sprint and their status, as you may remember the possible outcomes can be, "done", "blocked", "delayed", "not started", "not finished", or perhaps any of these with a comment and we want to keep the not started or not finished to a minimum.

Task ID	Task Name (User Story)	Status
009	take a course related to kindle self-publishing	Done
015	publish initial "About Me" section	Delayed, Done
016	complete the design of the home page	Done
017	prepare the initial structure for the book	Done
018	prepare a mockup of an app I would like to publish	Not Finished
014	make visual changes to the pages where articles are posted	Not Started

Before going through some of the User Stories for the next Sprint we should review the User Stories that are still ranked in the backlog but haven't been included in a planning or haven't yet been started. We should reassess each one of them to see if any of them are still a priority or not. See the changes on priorities in bold letters:

ID of Task	Topic or Project	As the Product Owner I want to...	so that...	and I will consider the task as done when...	Priority	Status	Stakeholder(s)
004	Industry Contributions	gather different channels or networks through which I can contribute	I can prepare the action plan according to these channels	I receive a list of channels that I will use to contribute	Low	Not Started	Product Owner
008	Industry Contributions	set connection features like email account, contact form and links to social media	we generate awareness, reach to more people and allow people to connect with us	we have at least 3 different ways for people to connect with us	Low	Not Started	Product Owner
010	Upskilling	do a course related to eBook marketing	we can leverage the knowledge to promote and divulge the book	course is completed and a list of marketing actions is drafted as next steps for the book's promotion	Medium	Not Started	Product Owner
011	Industry Contributions	add a newsletter form in at least two pages	visitors can register for updates	the form is visible and tested	Medium	Not Started	Product Owner
012	Industry Contributions	populate the blog with some relevant pictures	the blog starts having a visual effect in visitors	we see relevant pictures in the home page of the blog	Medium	Not Started	Product Owner
013	Industry Contributions	test all social media connections	we confirm all channels are reachable and visually appealing	we have linked Instagram, Facebook and Medium correctly and with some content posted	Medium	Not Started	Product Owner
014	Industry Contributions	make visual changes to the pages where articles are posted	anything we post is easy to read, interact and share	article pages are visible, shareable on social media, and disposition looks like other state of the art blogs	Medium	Not Started	Product Owner
018	Initiatives	prepare a mockup of an app I would like to publish	we can start drafting the features we want to include	we can see a mockup of the app we want to publish	High	Not Started	Product Owner
019	Initiatives	prepare a list of features for this initial version of the app	we can start developing these requirements with the software developers	we have defined at least the basic features of the app, sign-up, login and feed	Medium	Not Started	Product Owner

As you see we have changed a few priorities, this will allow us to focus more in what we think that right now will bring more value. Based on the first part of the meeting where we reviewed which User Stories would be completed and based on the updated product backlog, we can start adding new User Stories based on our new priorities and advances in our projects. See in the following table the User Stories we have decided to add right now.

ID of Task	Topic or Project	As the Product Owner I want to...	so that...	and I will consider the task as done when...	Priority	Status	Stakeholder(s)
020	Industry Contributions	draft a privacy policy	we are able to gather visitor information when the time comes	we publish a section with a privacy policy that is compliant to GDPR and allows us to gather information from users like email, name and social networks	Medium	Not Started	Product Owner
021	Industry Contributions	draft the initial chapter of the book as an introduction	we brief readers about the methodology and the book's goal	we deliver a word document, with a standard format that provides information about the methodology, the goal of the book, why I decided to write it, what do I want leaders to achieve with it	High	Not Started	Product Owner
022	Industry Contributions	find out the page sizes needed to publish the book in both eBook and Paperback editions	we are able to preview how the format and layout will look like	we deliver two templates in word format with typical sizes for books related to ours	High	Not Started	Product Owner
023	Industry Contributions	find a reliable anti-plagiarism checker	we are able to check each chapter for any plagiarism and add the necessary references when needed	we find an affordable anti-plagiarism checker, that is reliable, and that has great reviews online	Medium	Not Started	Product Owner

Sprint III – Sprint Review

<u>US 009 – take a course related to kindle self-publishing</u>

The definition of done for this task is quite simple, either the course is completed or not. But one important part is the main takeaways from the course about how to do an effective roll-out of the book, how to gather good reviews, and how to position the book in different book stores.

The key takeaways are:

- Having a free version for people to get a preview of the book
- Publishing the book in different stores rather than just the main ones
- The importance of a catchy title, catchy descriptions but also a strong index and appealing titles for each chapter
- Creating a whole eco-system around the book, perhaps a course or articles
- Leveraging author pages and affiliate marketing

<u>US 015 – publish initial "About Me" section</u>

The goal of this task was to publish an initial "About Me" section that allowed readers to understand the background of past contributions. It needed to be appealing and the structure should follow a story line, let's see the result.

I have detailed experience, background, tools and skills, but combined them with references and testimonials from people I have worked with or old bosses. A relevant comment about this User Story is that even though we have set up an initial prototype this is always subject to change. One of the things that I like about Agile, is the infinite game and every piece of work is always subject to improvements due to changes in the business environment.

Feedback: we need to polish the introduction, make it simple and impersonal, it might be smart to add a timeline, to see achievements over time, also changing the section credentials which might not add value to another one that shows better how I think or operate. There is also too much ego in the initial version, too much "me", "I", that needs to change too.

US 017 – prepare the initial structure for the book

The goal of this task was to set a structure that would allow us to start working immediately in the content, and the Product Owner's directions were that topics had to be practical, applicable, and as updated as possible in new leadership concepts where agile came in handy.

The structure we have prepared is totally practical, with Sprints instead of chapters. Between Sprints we have added different applicable cases where Scrum Masters add value as leaders of Agile Teams. See the initial draft below.

Let me give you some context

Case I. How to fall in love with Agile

Sprint I

Case II. Effective Stakeholder Management

Sprint II

Case III. Servant Leadership

Sprint III

Case IV. Tips for Daily Meetings

Sprint IV

Case V. Stop, evaluate the product backlog and consolidate

Conclusions

Feedback: we need to add a briefing chapter, also add a chapter where we track performance, we need to prove that the methodology actually helps teams perform better. We also need a chapter where we layout all the tools and meetings that Agile Frameworks leverage to deliver value, this will help readers to understand each Sprint better and follow the storyline.

As you might have realized this initial list has changed from the final structure of the book. I am glad it did, because when I started writing I realized I needed to give more context to any reader that wasn't familiar to these methodologies, and therefore added a few more chapters at the beginning to brief people that wanted to start using this methodology in their teams.

Sprint III – Sprint Retrospective

Let's try the Speed Car[14] retrospective where we list what is making us go faster, acting as an engine, and what is making us slower, acting as a parachute.

Engine – what makes us move faster	Parachute – what is slowing us down
Defining structures beforehand	Low value tasks
Sharing constant results of our work with the Product Owner	Lack of marketing knowledge
Asking for feedback in daily meetings	Research
Technical savviness	Documenting many of the things that we do
Training before starting a User Story, that will allow us to avoid common mistakes	Lack consistency, too many topics at the same time

If we thought the second column is really affecting us as a team we should create an action plan to tackle these issues. In this case we could pick a few and start addressing them. For instance, low value tasks might be outsourced, simple things like spelling checks, gathering examples of different ways to do what we want to do, this all can be outsourced to virtual assistants with the correct guidance. On another hand about the lack of consistency, we are wanting to do many things at the same time, so we might need a few sprints where we focus on User Stories related to one topic or two at most.

---

[14] Source: *Funretro, https://funretro.io/*

CASE V. OUTPUTS VS OUTCOMES

One of the main challenges that we are going to find ourselves with, is ensuring that we get the results we want from our Agile projects. When I was writing this book I realized that much of what I did was focusing on outputs, pieces of work that were going to be marketed with all the effort consumed in building the product but not ensuring the outcomes I expected from these pieces of work, the results. The outcomes of our work is going to differentiate us from a bunch of doers to actually being achievers, and here is where we need to change the approach of Agile. In current corporations this methodology is only applied in building products but not carrying the product forward to deliver the results we want. This chapter is exclusively about how I would start applying this same methodology to ensure I was following up after the roll-out of these products.

Let's see a few examples:

Output: Rolled out an App

Outcome: Achieved 5000+ downloads in less than a month or achieved 3000+ sign-ups in a month.

Outcomes can vary depending on the stage that we are in, sometimes our goals will be related to generate awareness, later to generate engagement, after to start monetizing, and so on and so forth. Let's use this chapter to see examples on how to apply the methodology to start executing on increasing the outcomes of one of our projects, the App.

Example of High-level goal definition:

Goal	Description	Success	Projects
Increase conversion in all funnels that lead	We will take actions in each phase of the conversion funnel for	Increase App downloads	Social - Instagram
			Social – Pinterest

---

to App download	each social media account, gain followers, gain visits, gain likes, gain clicks, etc.	in 10%	Social - Facebook
			Social – Word of mouth
Increase relevance of wines inside the App	We will upload wines that are more likely to be ordered in social situations, those that have loyal customers, and those that rank better on wine subscription services.	Increase wines saved as favorites by 20%	Restaurants recommendations (wines typically seen in good restaurants)
			Instagram (wines with followers and conversions)
			Wine prime subscription providers

Example of Product Backlog:

ID of Task	Topic or Project	As the Product Owner I want to...	so that...	and I will consider the task as done when...	Priority	Status
001	Social - Instagram	start following users from wine prime subscription providers	we convert them to our followers	we get 30 more followers by the end of this Sprint	High	Not Started
002	Social – Word of mouth	start reaching out to happy customers to show our appreciation for their loyalty	we get a good review from them in any known review provider (Trustpilot, google business, etc.)	we get two or three five-star reviews by the end of this Sprint	Medium	Not Started
003	Restaurants recommendations	gather wines from the menu of five top restaurants in Madrid	we get each wine's details and upload them to our App wine feed	we see at least 20 new wines from this source	Medium	Not Started

Add as a tool a performance-sprint tracking

Project	Sprint 1	Sprint 2	Sprint 3	...	Sprint N	Measurement	Goal
Social - Instagram	xxx	xxx	xxx	xxx	xxx	Sprint on Sprint (SoS)	New followers converted per Sprint
Social - Pinterest	xxx	xxx	xxx	xxx	xxx	Sprint on Sprint (SoS)	Number of monthly visitors (normalized metric in Pinterest) per sprint

Change the approach of the daily meetings

- Which target did I focus my work on yesterday? *I worked on increasing Instagram followers by following target users gathered from wine subscription services*
- Which target will I focus my work on today? *I will start working on relevant content to increase the number of monthly visitors to Pinterest accounts*
- What problems are we running into when taking action? *If I follow too many people in a short period of time, we might get our Instagram account blocked temporarily*
- Metrics up so far? *This week we have achieved 20 new followers up to this day, which give us a rate of around 6 new followers per day*

Change Sprint Reviews for Performance Meetings

Besides the changes in the way we define our User Stories and the definition of "Done", there should be a specific approach for Sprint Reviews. Instead of going through what has been done during the Sprint, the team actually goes through the different actions taken in previous Sprints and the results of these, the actions taken in this Sprint, and set new goals for the next one.

Project	User Story	Actions taken in this Sprint	Sprint outcomes	Cumulative achievements
Social - Instagram	start following users from wine prime subscription providers	xxx	xxx	xxxx
Social - Pinterest	xxx	xxx	xxx	xxxx

SPRINT IV

Sprint IV – Planning

After the Sprint Review from Sprint III we might need to add new User Stories that implement the feedback gathered from that session. Right now the Product Backlog, if we filter by Priority Medium or High, looks like this:

ID of Task	Topic or Project	As the Product Owner I want to...	so that...	and I will consider the task as done when...	Priority	Status	Stakeholder(s)
010	Upskilling	do a course related to eBook marketing	we can leverage the knowledge to promote and divulge the book	course is completed and a list of marketing actions is drafted as next steps for the book's promotion	Medium	Not Started	Product Owner
011	Industry Contributions	add a newsletter form in at least two pages	visitors can register for updates	the form is visible and tested	Medium	Not Started	Product Owner
012	Industry Contributions	populate the blog with some relevant pictures	the blog starts having a visual effect in visitors	we see relevant pictures in the home page of the blog	Medium	Not Started	Product Owner
013	Industry Contributions	test all social media connections	we confirm all channels are reachable and visually appealing	we have linked Instagram, Facebook and Medium correctly and with some content posted	Medium	Not Started	Product Owner
014	Industry Contributions	make visual changes to the pages where articles are posted	anything we post is easy to read, interact and share	article pages are visible, shareable on social media, and disposition looks like other state of the art blogs	Medium	Not Started	Product Owner
018	Initiatives	prepare a mockup of an app I would like to publish	we can start drafting the features we want to include	we can see a mockup of the app we want to publish	High	Not Started	Product Owner
019	Initiatives	prepare a list of features for this initial version of the app	we can start developing these requirements with the software developers	we have defined at least the basic features of the app, sign-up, login and feed	Medium	Not Started	Product Owner
020	Industry Contributions	draft a privacy policy	we are able to gather visitor information when the time comes	we publish a section with a privacy policy that is compliant to GDPR and allows us to gather information from users like email, name and social networks	Medium	Not Started	Product Owner
021	Industry Contributions	draft the initial chapter of the book as an introduction	we brief readers about the methodology and the book's goal	we deliver a word document, with a standard format that provides information about the methodology, the goal of the book, why I decided to write it, what do I want leaders to achieve with it	High	Not Started	Product Owner
022	Industry Contributions	find out the page sizes needed to publish the book in both eBook and Paperback editions	we are able to preview how the format and layout will look like	we deliver two templates in word format with typical sizes for books related to ours	High	Not Started	Product Owner

Let's add now the User Stories that result from the feedback gathered in the Sprint Review.

ID of Task	Topic or Project	As the Product Owner I want to...	so that...	and I will consider the task as done when...	Priority	Status	Stakeholder(s)
024	Industry Contributions	polish the introduction from the "About Me" section in the website	it is more personal; it connects better with the audience and helps spreading a message or perception	we see the updated version published at the website	High	Not Started	Product Owner
025	Industry Contributions	remove credentials section and replace for contributions timeline	we provide visibility on contributions to the industry rather than just titles or certificates	we see a version of the timeline published in the website	High	Not Started	Product Owner
026	Industry Contributions	add a chapter where we layout all the tools and meetings that Agile Frameworks leverage to deliver value	readers get to know the artifacts of the methodology before seeing how we apply them	we include the chapter in the structure of the book and we actually draft an initial version of it, including, tools, meetings and roles	Medium	Not Started	Product Owner
027	Industry Contributions	create an author page	the book is combined to testimonials and articles	we publish an initial author page in Amazon	Low	Not Started	Product Owner
028	Industry Contributions	create a free version of the book	potential readers can preview the content of the book and decide whether they like it or not	we draft an initial version with no more than 20 pages that explain, what do we want to achieve with the book, how the methodology can help teams across the organization, how to leverage the framework in leadership roles	Low	Not Started	Product Owner

The priority of each task has been defined based on the status of our projects, some make sense to start right now, others make sense to start in future Sprints where we already have a better idea of what the core projects will look like. For instance, there is no point in drafting an initial free version of the book if we still haven't started writing the book, or creating the author page might be something we do after we have started writing a few chapters of the book.

Now that we have updated the Product Backlog and set priorities let's start planning the Sprint. Since there is a bank holiday on 25/12 we can do two things, either extend the Sprint one day, or as a better practice, simply reduce the capacity, which is what we are going to do here:

Sprint Goal: Make changes to the blog and start moving forward with book chapters
Sprint End-Date: 27/12

		Capacity (in hours)	27
Task ID	Task Name (User Story)	Team Estimation (hours)	Capacity Left
xxx	xxx	xxx	xxx

Let's start including User Stories and see some examples on how we estimate them:

<u>US 018 – prepare a mockup of an app I would like to publish</u>

This task has been carried from the previous Sprint, the goal was to start preparing a mockup design of an app that we would like to publish. In order to prepare this mockup have need to do some research, find a topic that was enjoyable but that had a market, also a topic in which I could generate the corresponding marketing around it to ensure there are downloads.

- Is there any analysis that needs to be done beforehand and that can delay the task? Decide a topic that I felt interested about and liked. This is a side project and I want it to be about something I enjoy, but also needs to be easy to market, which means it needs to be a B2C app, focused on users.
- Are there any dependencies on other teams that need to be untangled? No
- Is there any complexity hidden in this task or any risk of not having reliable sources of information on time? Not that we know of, it is probably going to be an easy exercise.
- What does the Product Owner want to see and in which format? A mockup design of a simple App with the features for each view
- Is there an impact of these tasks in any other teams or current processes (or systems)? No

Let's see the list of tasks contained by this User Story, since it's an app at its initial stage any decision made now is subject to change. This is really important to understand if we want to start moving forward. There will be margin to change the App's name, to create new features or views, but for now we need to start building a prototype with what we have:

Change	Estimation (hrs.)
Research and decide topic of interest and marketable	4
Title of the App	2
What is the App's functionality about?	1
Main features	2
Main views	2

In the past Sprint we were able to start researching about a topic of interest and marketable, therefore we will only assign seven hours of capacity to this User Story in our planning for Sprint IV.

US 021 – draft the initial chapter of the book as an introduction

This User Story will be the initial chapter of the book, we have already got a title for it "Let me give you some context", and I like it, so we are going to keep it. Now we need to decide how we want to communicate the message we want our readers to absorb. If it's the first time we are writing a book chapter it's really hard to know how much time will be spent. So we are going to estimate the time writing it but also the time that we will spend rewriting it and rereading it, which is something very likely to happen in these initial stages.

Task	Estimation (hrs.)
Provide context	0.5
Why this methodology?	1
What is the goal of the book?	0.5
Why do I feel it will help you?	1
What can you expect from this reading?	1

US 026 – add a chapter where we layout all the tools and meetings that Agile Frameworks leverage to deliver value

This chapter is extremely important since we will brief the reader in all the tools, artifacts, and meetings that the methodology leverages to run smoothly. Let's see the list of tasks included:

Task	Estimation (hrs.)
Agile's origins	0.5
Agile's values	0,5
Roles	2
Meetings	3
Tools	1

References	0,5
Proofreading	0,5

After having estimated all tasks, let's see how the planning for this Sprint looks like:

Sprint Goal: Make changes to the blog and start moving forward with book chapters

Sprint End-Date: 27/12

		Capacity (in hours)	27
Task ID	**Task Name (User Story)**	**Team Estimation (hours)**	**Capacity Left**
018	prepare a mockup of an app I would like to publish	7	20
021	draft the initial chapter of the book as an introduction	4	16
022	find out the page sizes needed to publish the book in both eBook and Paperback editions	2	14
024	polish the introduction from the "About Me" section in the website	3	11
025	remove credentials section and replace for contributions timeline	6	5
020	draft a privacy policy	4	1
026	add a chapter where we layout all the tools and meetings that Agile Frameworks leverage to deliver value	8	-7

Sprint IV – Daily Meetings

Day 2.

- What did I do yesterday? *Yesterday I was able to decide what was going to be the App's name, we will call it "The Wine App". It will allow people to share their favorite wines, see their friends' favorite wines and share wine suggestions with them*
- What will I spend my time on today? *I will start working on the main features MVP to submit to our freelance developers*
- What is blocking me from completing this task on time? *we need to start engaging with different freelance android developers to understand budget or submit a RFP, to start vetting them and the*

reviews each one has to see which one suits better our budget and requirements. Depending on these we might need to change the features list, if a developer finds a certain feature very complex we might get overcharged so we need to decide which features a developer can do in a constrained amount of time

Based on this Daily we could decide either to add a new User Story to the Sprint that aims to perform the necessary research of Android developers that are within budget and can do a good job, or we could add this user story to the next sprint and just focus on outlining the features we want and later deciding which ones are going to be prioritized in the first development cycle. Both could be good solutions, but the first one could block this first User Story and introduce some inefficiency in the Sprint, therefore in this case we are going to stick with getting this User Story done and creating another one to vet a developer for the Next Sprint.

Day 4.
- What did I do yesterday? *I finished the mockup designs of the different views that the app is going to have, also I started working on the initial chapter of the book, called "Let me give you some context" in which we will brief readers about the book and about why we are publishing it*
- What will I spend my time on today? *I will keep on working on the initial chapter of the book*
- What is blocking me from completing this task on time? *nothing, right now*

Day 6.
- What did I do yesterday? *I was able to download different templates with their corresponding sizes for both paperback and eBook editions, allowing us to start adapting the format of the book to the corresponding sizes. I also started updating the "About me" section of the webpage, including more outcomes in professional experiences and polishing the brief initial introduction about me as a professional*
- What will I spend my time on today? *mainly removing the credentials section from the page and replacing it with a timeline of contributions*

- What is blocking me from completing this task on time? *I cannot configure a horizontal timeline, and a vertical one simply makes the page too long, I might need to look for another plugin*

Sprint IV – Refinement Meeting

The agenda for this Sprint's Refinement Meeting is the following:

- We will go through the tasks that should be delivered by the end of the Sprint and realign expectations. Also we will talk about any roadblocks that have stopped us from finishing or starting any of the tasks in our planning. – 15 minutes
- Add some of the new tasks planned for the next Sprint so that the team can make the necessary due diligence to provide precise estimations on the planning meeting. – 20 minutes

Let's start with the tasks that ought to be delivered by the end of the Sprint and their status, as you may remember the possible outcomes can be, "done", "blocked", "delayed", "not started", "not finished", or perhaps any of these with a comment and we want to keep the not started or not finished to a minimum.

Task ID	Task Name (User Story)	Status
018	prepare a mockup of an app I would like to publish	Done
021	draft the initial chapter of the book as an introduction	Done
022	find out the page sizes needed to publish the book in both eBook and Paperback editions	Done
024	polish the introduction from the "About Me" section in the website	Done
025	remove credentials section and replace for contributions timeline	Done
020	draft a privacy policy	Not finished, delayed
026	add a chapter where we layout all the tools and meetings that Agile Frameworks leverage to deliver value	Not started

Since the past Sprint we went through the whole backlog and reassessed priorities. In this Refinement Meeting we are just going to add a few new User

Stories in order to allow the team to prepare for the next planning meeting. We want to start working on the rest of the User Stories that have been carried from other Sprints so we are just going to add these two:

ID of Task	Topic or Project	As the Product Owner I want to...	so that...	and I will consider the task as done when...	Priority	Status	Stakeholder(s)
029	Initiatives	vet and choose an Android Developer on a budget	we can start developing the MVP of our App	we have chosen two or three developers, with great reviews from demanding clients (usually in Europe or US), and have received a quote for an initial MVP	High	Not Started	Product Owner
030	Industry Contributions	vet and choose a proofreader on a budget	we can start sending chapters to double check and correct	we have chosen two or three proofreaders, with great reviews from demanding clients (usually in Europe or US), and have received an initial quote per 500 words	Medium	Not Starter	Product Owner

Sprint IV – Sprint Review

US 018 – prepare a mockup of an app I would like to publish

The goal of this task was to define the name of the App, the features, and prepare the different views we were going to develop for the initial version that we would publish. Let's resume the outcomes of all the work done, the name of the app is "The Wine App", it will be initially built for Android and will allow users to: create an account, login, save favorite wines, rate wines, share wines, and see the wines their friends have saved. Let's see a few snapshots of the designs of the initial version, including splash screen, sign-up, feed, and friend feed.

US 021 – draft the initial chapter of the book as an introduction

The goal of this task was to deliver an initial chapter with a standard formatting that provided information about the methodology, the goal of the book, why did I decide to write it, and what do I want leaders to achieve with it. Let's see what the initial chapter looks like:

LET ME GIVE YOU SOME CONTEXT

During the last year I have tried to apply the principles of a very well-known IT methodology to some of my personal projects to see how it felt and how much I was able to get done, the goal was not only to try a different approach to handle personal projects but also to prove that this methodology could be used in many different areas of any company that feels the need to achieve better results, valuable outcomes, great team spirit and strong sense of satisfaction.

Why do I think this methodology can help in different areas rather than just being a typical methodology for software development? Because of its principles, the way they fit the current reality, the way they apply to modern organizations, and because it has worked in different situations, for instance, Operational teams or Sales teams. Agile is a very dynamic methodology, usually underestimated by the industry since it is only known to be used in IT teams but it is extremely powerful to manage teams in different areas or departments that liaise with stakeholders, have a changing environment, and want to handle changing priorities quickly and effectively. The fun part is that these principles can also be applied to modern lifestyle, and this is how the book can help you infer the potential of Agile methodology to handle both personal and professional projects, regardless the size.

I hope this book helps both you and your team. We are using real situations that different professionals face during their careers in order to introduce the context and be able to infer the concept, to exemplify the project we will use personal goals to which we will apply Agile principles to get them moving forward and throughout the book I will share materials and templates that are useful for any team that wants to run this methodology. Product Backlog template, Daily Meetings script, ROI and performance calculation. The goal is to show examples on how they can be used so that it is easy to apply in a business environment.

Between chapters we include some extra concepts, tips or interesting applications that are really useful when applying Agile methodologies and that have been learnt and proven through experience, but that are not part of the core knowledge of the methodology, for instance, smart stakeholder management, managing conflicts inside the Agile team, dealing with budget, improving team's image with stakeholders, etc. At the end of the book you will find great material and tools to use to get your team running in Agile and, last but not least, a lot of ideas for effective retrospective meetings depending on the context and situation that your team is living in a specific moment.

Feedback: we need to make clear what we want leaders to achieve with it, we might need to remove the last paragraph and adapt it to the final structure of the book, we have to change the starting paragraph to provide a more empathic introduction.

As you may have realized the final version (in this same book) has differed a little bit from this draft and the reason is simple, in this framework, the final product can and should be adapted constantly to meet new requirements that our environment sets in front of us.

Sprint IV – Sprint Retrospective

The retrospective we have chosen for this Sprint is the SWOT Analysis[15] which identifies Strengths, Weaknesses, Opportunities, and Threats.

Strengths – what are we doing well	Weaknesses – what we could do better
Moving forward	Inconsistency, we want to do many different things at the same time, each task has a different nature from the one before and that introduces inefficiency
Starting to focus on tangible deliveries	
Working smarter to identify what needs to be done by us and what needs to be done by others	Need more focus on outcomes versus outputs

[15] Source: *Funretro, https://funretro.io/*

Within budget	Low capacity impedes gaining momentum
Opportunities – what in our environment we can start leveraging	**Threats – with the weaknesses above what risks do we see**
Since much of what we are doing is linked to professional development we can start focusing our User Stories to this goal Since there are already tangible deliveries, we can start testing them to see the reaction of the market, for instance publishing articles based on chapters of the book Identify tasks to outsource, those that don't add much value and are taking time, are repetitive and in general have nothing to do with parts in which spending our time is important to achieve the results we want	Lack of consistency might kill our productivity Focusing on deliveries over outcomes might stall us from testing our product in the market before investing a lot of time in ineffective tasks Challenges when outsourcing, confidentiality, vetting our collaborators, overpricing

PERFORMANCE TRACKING

There are many ways in which we can track performance from different perspectives. Even though there are official ways in which this can be done, I am going to focus on practical ways in which Scrum Masters or leaders can assess areas in which the whole team can improve when working under this framework.

Team Satisfaction

Team satisfaction is becoming one of the most important indicators of wellbeing and performance of a team. In many companies it's actually becoming part of the leadership's goals and targets. Agile Methodologies have a natural tendency to lead to higher motivation and team satisfaction, still understanding how the team is doing can be a great source of input for Scrum Masters and leaders in general.

What is the problem? If the team is feeling frustrated, we need to understand what is happening, the root cause. Is the pace too intense? Are we being too aggressive when estimating? Are we communicating effectively? Is there any weird dynamic going on between members of the team? Are our team members working correctly with stakeholders? Are our team members doing what they best know what to do?

How to address it? We should send team satisfaction surveys every once in a while, ensuring anonymity, and making sure people are encouraged to speak up in a constructive manner to understand if we need to act on something. Also, the retrospective meetings are a great place to sense how the team is feeling, dropping in retrospective motivational questions can help the Scrum Master identify any situation that is bringing team motivation down.

Expectations Management and Estimation Issues

Understanding how the team is estimating User Stories and the level of reliability of these estimations can help the Scrum Master address expectation management issues or Product Backlog issues.

What is the problem? If the Product Owner is not providing enough details to estimate or if the team is estimating incorrectly this can lead to trust issues between the Product Owner and the team, lack of alignment between the team and stakeholders that are impacted by our User Stories being delivered on time or not, budget deviations, deeper problems as lack of technical ability or lack of understanding of the complexity of our products or processes. On the other hand, if the team is estimating correctly, but tasks are too complex or need more technical discussions we need to facilitate these discussions and support these discussions in a way that the correct questions are made before estimating.

How do we address it? Simple, by adding another column in the Planning Template with the final time spent in each User Story.

Task ID	Task Name (User Story)	Team Estimation (hours)	Final Dedication
018	prepare a mockup of an app I would like to publish	7	8
021	draft the initial chapter of the book as an introduction	4	4

Every once in a while, check how many User Stories were on time, how many were done ahead of time and how many were delayed from the total. This way it will be easier to identify if the methodology needs to start facilitating the team in doing more research before estimating or even provide a better framework to estimate.

Product Backlog Progression and Performance

Setting some trackers into our product Backlog could allow us to understand if we are performing well as a team, if we are working with direction, or if we need some focus.

What is the problem? If we are moving slowly down the Product Backlog and not completing projects this can be a sign of lack of focus, lack of resources, or lack of definition. Being able to assess the evolution of how we have been progressing through the product backlog can help reduce the User Stories that are submitted and that aren't adding value, the number of topics we are carrying at the same time, or even redefining the scope of our projects before it turns into a structural issue inside our teams.

How to address it? Simple, calculating the number of User Stories that are marked as Done over the total number of User Stories in the Product Backlog and watching how they evolve over time.

Project Dispersion

As teams start using this framework and improving in the process, there is always some risk of including new projects and new streams of work because of external pressure or stakeholders' needs. I am a strong believer of multi-tasking, but I also have been extremely frustrated when I was doing so many things and all of them of a different nature. In a modern organization you can find yourself working through spreadsheets or with numbers in the morning, preparing a presentation during lunch time, revamping a process in the evening, and attending to high-level meetings at the end of the day. Even though these are linked to each other in certain ways, sometimes multi-tasking can result in a lack of focus and inefficiency when moving from one task to another.

What is the problem? If we are getting dispersed this can have an impact in the ROI of the projects, an impact on the quality of our work. If we are juggling with multiple projects at the same time and feeling overwhelmed, we might need to reassess priorities or move in time initiatives that are not urgent or that don't provide enough value. It's a tradeoff call that the Product Owner needs to make but the Scrum Master might need to raise if no one is looking carefully.

How to address it? Calculating the number of projects and progression for each, calculating the number of different projects handled by each team member who worked User Stories over the last few sprints. Anything that shows team members are working on tasks from more than two different projects in the same Sprint can be ineffective.

Stakeholder Satisfaction

Working with stakeholders can be challenging but also rewarding when the team is able to deliver to its eco-system. Being able to keep up with the needs of our stakeholders whilst achieving our goals is important as to how the team is perceived within the organization and how it contributes to the business goals.

What is the problem? There are two kinds of issues here, the satisfaction or lack of it from our stakeholders, and the balance between their goals and our goals as a team. If we are prioritizing pleasing stakeholders but putting in jeopardy our own goals, or if we are focusing too much in our goals and not delivering to stakeholders that are being negatively impacted, we want to act on it and balance out our dedication and priorities.

How do we address it? Sending out internal CSat surveys and calculating Product backlog performance could help us understand if we are too consumed by our stakeholders or if we are too focused on ourselves and not working in a collaborative manner. If CSat results are low and our goals are being achieved we might need to start thinking about our eco-system, if CSat results are high but we are not achieving our own goals we might need to push back a little bit. If both are high we can assume we are finding a good balance or if both are low we might have a real issue there.

CONCLUSION

Juggling with stakeholders, people management, releases, deliveries, commitments, and targets is something that many of us are going to face throughout our careers. When I decided to write this book I wanted to create awareness of a methodology that has been traditionally linked to IT environments and that carries a huge potential to any team that works in high paced, demanding environments that require constantly delivering and gathering feedback. From a practical perspective many teams are working in this way but not many of them are applying these methodologies to work in a methodical and structured manner to ensure goals are met and the process is smooth. If you look back in the book, between Sprints it didn't look as if we were doing great things, but after several iterations you are reading a final product of this methodology, this same book, that was included as a project for one high-level goal defined at the beginning.

What I want the reader to understand is that if by applying Agile Methodologies a few hours per day during weekdays, allowed me to publish a functioning App called "The Wine App", a book called "An Agile Life" and all the eco-system around it. Imagine what leaders can do applying these methodologies to their teams with way more talent than a single person and way more capacity, and probably more budget. You will be able to work with several stakeholders at the same time, increase the pace in which your team delivers, improve satisfaction, gather feedback in a structured manner, follow through commitment and, in general, feel that you effectively drive things forward in iterative, ambiguous environments that are subject to external changes constantly.

Thinking about my target audience I struggled to define who was an ideal reader of this book, since it could serve a typical leader in a corporation, or a manager in a startup, or a young professional that likes initiating side-projects that help them disconnect from their nine to five job; or even those that have their own company and need to feel they understand what is going on when the company is growing so quickly.

I really hope you have enjoyed this read, and I am open to answering any of your questions with no strings attached, just feel free to reach out by email or LinkedIn. I will gladly help you in understanding what you need based on what you want to achieve and how to get there.

Help me spread this methodology by leaving a review if you have liked the book!

COMMITMENT TO QUALITY

The goal of this chapter is to provide transparency to readers about the actions taken to ensure that quality information and valuable experience are delivered to anybody that wants to successfully implement these methodologies in their teams.

Certified Practitioner

As a certified practitioner I possess the credentials provided by Scrum.org that are obtained with the corresponding experience and exams.

Continuous improvement

This book is updated based on the feedback provided by experts, proofreading and focus groups where people can openly talk about what they liked and didn't like.

The book also has a feedback system in place where readers can rate different chapters and provide feedback through surveys, all of this is taken into consideration when making changes.

State of the art content

This book is not theorical, actually all the theory is contained in one or two chapters, the rest of the content is purely practical, content obtained through valuable experience in different industries, companies and cultures.

I am constantly engaging with people from different parts of Europe and US to get new ideas and information on improvements on people management, stakeholder management, and performance improvement.

Personalized experience

In this book there are several ways to connect with me and even schedule a meeting so that you can ask your questions, the goal here is that once you have had to read it you feel free to forward me any doubts or questions you have on implementing this methodology in your teams and projects.

ABOUT THE AUTHOR

Vishal Wadhwani is a professional with more than 7 years combined experience in Operations and Technology. He comes from a very diverse environment, with cultural influences from India, UK and Spain. He has worked for top players in their corresponding industries, using the latest technology, and leveraging the most updated leadership techniques to effectively manage both agile and non-agile teams in cross-regional and multi-cultural environments.

Throughout his career he has worked in a variety of projects related to top-tier technology, cultural, and digital transformation. During his tenure he has been able to observe how different project management techniques impact project rollouts and team motivation. The rising importance of effective project frameworks that ensure motivation and performance inspired him to write this book.

Amazon Author Page - amazon.com/author/vishalww

LinkedIn Page - linkedin.com/in/vishalwadhwani

Contact the author - vk.wadhwani@gmail.com

Web Page - millennialworkforce.space

Printed in Great Britain
by Amazon